MW01178876

Prodigal Son

Prodigal Son

One Man's Spiritual Journey

Rev. Larry J. Goodnough

Copyright © 2011 by Rev. Larry J. Goodnough.

ISBN:	Softcover	978-1-4628-9168-9
	Ebook	978-1-4628-9169-6

All rights reserved. No part of this book may be reproduced or transmitted in any form or by any means, electronic or mechanical, including photocopying, recording, or by any information storage and retrieval system, without permission in writing from the copyright owner.

This book was printed in the United States of America.

To order additional copies of this book, contact:
Xlibris Corporation
1-888-795-4274
www.Xlibris.com
Orders@Xlibris.com
97665

Contents

CHAPTER ONE

"The Early Years"

MY FATHER CAME home from the war wounded with shrapnel; anxious to leave his five years over-seas absence behind him. I was born in Orillia, Ontario on October 3, 1947 (Transitus of St. Francis). My father told me they tried to conceive for five years before they had me their first-born. My dad got a job working at General Motors in Oshawa. He was a painter on the factory line. He built a home there. I was very young but I can still remember he used to pull me up and down between floors in a five-gallon pail as he was building the house next to the railway tracks. I used to sit on a huge rock there most of the day just looking around. I remember a young girl who would come and sit with me; I didn't know who it was but I realize in the picture it was Lana. I remember a promotion for the new Wonder Bread. It seems I was a curious child and was always getting in trouble. I rode my red tricycle to school before I was of age to go, and to their surprise discovered me sitting in one of the classrooms. Once, my dad had to come home from work to fish me out of the heating ducts that I had crawled down into. My poor mother had a fit when once I was walking across a set of four train tracks when a train came from one direction and another came from the other. She watched in horror as the two trains passed. I dove between the two tracks and bounced around but was unhurt. My poor mother thought that was the end of me! It was said that as a child I used to sit on my mother's lap all the time, my mother tenderly showing me love and affection.

When it seemed that all was finally going well, my mother began to show signs of mental illness; fear and anxiety began to settle within her. She would close all the curtains and wear sunglasses in the house; she would stay in her bedroom most of the day and rarely went out. If she went out she would return and re-live each moment. My dad lost his job at General Motors as he increasingly stayed home to look after mom, and eventually he lost the home he built.

We moved to Wyebridge, Ontario because my mother's relatives lived there. We lived on my grandparent's farm along with my grandmother Livina who chewed white peppermint candies all the time. My grandfather was a strict man. I remember that he walked slightly bent over. My grandfather's last name was Busch and came from German decent; his father came over in 1914 and began a bakery in Toronto from what I got from my research. My grandmother's decent was Scottish. Her last name was McLean.

The farm had nothing indoors. We spent the night by kerosene lamps. No television, no radio, except for one that had old batteries attached to it, I never saw it work! We had a party line telephone with rings to identify you. No one used it except for emergencies. We pumped our water from a well, and I spent many hours freezing in the outhouse, reading and looking at the bras in the Simpson Sears Catalogues. I spent a lot of time alone on that farm. I was always getting into mischief. Once, I stole my grandfather's double barrel shotgun and two shells and went out into the bush to hunt! I saw a bird, pulled both triggers and went flying on my butt. I could see nothing of the bird but feathers. Once when the creek turned into a swift flowing river in the spring, I went down there to play. Grandpa's Lassie dog, Collie, got in front of me and would not let me go near the danger of the fast running water and barked until my father came to get me. The strong current surely would have taken me away! I love dogs to this day! My grandfather took me out to a field when he blew up some stumps with dynamite. I don't have a lot of memories about my grandfather except that he was strict and he criticized my father for not disciplining me more or for not making me work all the time.

My father bought me a BB gun, against my mother's wishes. I shot a sparrow, and as it lay dying on the ground, with my father beside me, there was a moment of truth; we both felt a shame within our hearts. Dad was in the Queen's Own Rifles. At that moment, he remembered and imparted on to me the horror of war and the shame of killing. The war must have taken a toll on him. Upon his return he didn't recognize his own wife when he got off the train because she wore makeup and he thought she was a hooker! He talked of the Zider Zee in Holland and how he would like to return there someday. He said there was a family that treated him good. Dad just wanted to forget the war. Dad once told me: "Believe only half of what you see; and nothing of what you hear!" Dad never had any friends from the army or any friends and he never joined the Canadian Legion. He had a hard time settling down after the war and I remember him talking about the Boyd Gang. The Boyd Gang was a notorious criminal gang based in Toronto. Perhaps, it was his way of expressing his thoughts of discouragement and asking himself what did he spend five years of his life fighting for? The only winners of the war were the rich! He now had lost his job and a good income and was now forced to live with mom's family. It was only when I was older that my dad would tell me his experience of the War. I pushed him once to tell me more about his experiences and he told me a horrible tale. One I kept to myself! He told me this story as not to question him anymore about the war. He didn't want to go there in his mind and I never asked him again. We took the gun back to the store and I have never owned a gun since.

I remember good experiences on the farm. I wandered around the farm and enjoyed being alone with the nature and countryside. I attended a one-room school. I couldn't wait till school was over. I would watch the clock each agonizing thud of the clock seemed for eternity. The teacher decided we would have a soapbox derby. My father helped me build a soapbox car, it was big and heavy and I lugged it all the way to school, I was a strong kid. There was no one able to push me in the cart, so I got a small kid to be my driver and I pushed my cart faster than the other boys, and won. I remember as a child I was always singing. I remember coming home from school singing, "You are my sunshine". I recall coming up the long driveway to the farm with the smell of Lilac trees lining the way. Later in my life my dad commented how they would know I was coming home from school for they could hear me singing!

Walking home required that I walk a good distance down the country roads. Some times I was late coming home because I would stop to watch the tadpoles in the creek so I would take the short cut through the bush. As the rays of light began to fade through the trees I felt a presence in those woods, I had a strong sense that I was not alone. I have never felt I was alone! I have felt lonely in my life but I have always felt that I was not alone. The closes thing I had to religion was once my mother took me to a Baptist Church in Midland.

My mother had a life before she began getting sick. I knew she also was enlisted in the army and spent a time out west. She surprised me one day when she went next door to the Fagan farm; and she played the piano like she was a professional. Donna, the Fagan girl, told me my mother once played the piano for the community dances when she was younger. My father also had music in his blood, he played the mouth organ. His family was from the Salvation Army tradition and was active in the brass band. I heard dad blow the trumpet once.

Someone got the great idea to take my mother to the Penetang Mental Hospital and she was given shock treatment. After that, my poor mother was afraid to go to the hospital and had all of her remaining children at home. I helped my father deliver a baby by oil lamp, which I believe was Richard. I would have been seven or eight years of age. I held the umbilical cord, while my dad cut the cord and tied it. My dad told me, if I let go of this end of the cord your mom will die and if you let go of the other end the baby would die. I still remember squeezing my thumbs and index finger so hard my fingers went numb. After Richard was born we moved to Toronto. I remember my grandmother Sarah Ann; her maiden name was McCullough. Her mother's maiden name was Murphy. My father, father's name was Percy Goodnough, his father's name was George Henry Goodenough. His wife's maiden name was Ada Scholes. Percy emigrated from England and lost the "e" in Goodnough. My grandmother Sarah was a short woman, she immigrated to Canada from Ireland as a teenager and worked in a canning factory in Grimsby, Ontario. I liked her! She used to visit us and would bring me something each time she came. Once, when she didn't bring me anything, I asked her if she brought me something and her response was: "Do you only like me when I have something for you?" The only other time I remember her was when I visited her in the hospital as a teenager, before she died. Last thing I remember of her telling me was: "Don't steal anything around here because they're watching you here!" What she didn't know, I had learned my lesson about stealing! When I was young I stole a bag of toys soldiers from a supermarket in Toronto. My father made me take them back to the manager and admit to stealing them. My dad was a little cruel at times, but I believe that everything he did was for my own good.

In Toronto I became friends with a minister's son and we used to play in his father's church. I remember the smell of the old books. We had a hard time. I remember my sister, Lana, and myself getting very sick with a high fever at one place we lived. We lived next door to a bakery plant. I felt justified to climb through a window of the plant and steal bread and cakes. At another place, I stole big cans of soup, from the back of a store. I remember an Italian gang of kids who would poke me with swords made from coat hangers. My dad told me to remember the little bee, people are afraid of the bee because of his stinger. So, I filled my pocket full of small rocks and would peg each the gang on the head as I saw them, they became afraid of me. I was called to the principal's office and my dad came to my defense! We moved a lot. My dad got me a job selling newspapers at the Toronto Exhibition. I couldn't figure out why all the other kids were riding the amusements but not me, so I spent all the money I got for the newspapers on the rides. Why couldn't I ride? Why were others privileged?

I don't know how we ended up in family court; I heard rumors that it was my father's relatives in Toronto who called the Children's Aide on us. I remember a couple of workers came to our house and dad threw them off the front porch. The children's Aide took my family to court. I vaguely remember my mother in the courtroom and the sadness in her. The next thing I knew I was taken away from my family. I was about nine years old when the Children's Aid Services stepped in and took all of us children away. I remember it to this day, a couple of police officers came up a long set of stairs and took baby Richard right out of my mother's arms. I remember the Social Worker dropping me off at the Children's Aide playground and I watched my mother and father, with tears in their eyes peering through the small oval window of that old black car. I watched until it pulled out of sight with a pain in my heart that I can still feel to this day. To this day when I see a mother or father leave their children it brings tears to my eyes. All of my family was gone. I lay in bed crying that night, and the night worker came up and told me to shut up. I learned to be quiet and turn within myself, and not to trust. I didn't settle in well. The courts sent me to a holding center called Christie Street. It was a cruel place and I grew up pretty fast in there. The boys would all sit on a big desk in a huge hall;

it reminds me of an army barracks. At night some of the boys tried to sexually assault me! What had I done to be taken away from my family and put in jail? I was sent back to the Children's Aide Center. My father made a visit to see me there at the Children's Aide and told me to misbehave and they would let me come home.

I often wondered where and how my sister and brothers were doing? I wanted to be a family again. I remember swinging on the pipes in the basement of the Children's Aide and crashing through a ping-pong table and splitting my head open and getting stitches. I was a scrapper in school and would simply flip those who would fight with me, over my back to the ground. I spent a lot of time in the principal's office painting garbage cans. I remember once in class a girl sent me a note and asked me if I wanted to have sex! I had no idea want to do! I said yes, and we met under a bridge and lay upon each other with our clothes on. One of the kids from the Children's Aide saw me from the top of the bridge and interrupted us, and when I walked to him to go home with him he kicked me on my funny bone in my arm. I remember how much it hurt. I couldn't figure why he would do that, perhaps he was jealous that a girl showed me attention. I also remember going to a Sunday school for a couple weeks in a row. We could earn candy if we remembered a scripture verse. I was taught John 3:16 "For God so loved the world that He gave his son that whosoever believeth in Him shall not perish but have eternal life." And "Seek and you shall find." Those would be the only scriptures I would know until I became thirty years old.

When I was eight years old, I was a ward of the Children's Aid Society. In those days there were not many, if any persons I admired. I remember going to a movie theatre with some of the other boys from the Aid. While we were waiting for the theater to open I was humiliated by those boys who where supposed to be my friends.

The movie that day was the Jules Verne classic: "Twenty Thousand Leagues Under the Sea". I remember coming into the theatre from the cold into a warm environment, sitting by myself. I found a comfort away from the others that I enjoy to this day! When the movie began I became James Mason, I was Captain Nemo. At a time in my life when I was powerless Captain Nemo was not. He destroyed the evil men who where selling their gun powder and he sunk their ships with the submarine the "Nautilus". Captain Nemo created a world away from the bullies of this world in his beautiful under water city. Captain Nemo did what we all wish we could do. He took control of his own destiny life and created a world away from conformity and injustice.

My feelings about him and what he stood for has not changed, in fact he inspires me to this day! It is not possible to create a world like Jules Verne's but it is possible to create ones own world! In some cases it means to totally deny the one created for us. For others, the conformity provides a structure to fulfill oneself. It is very important what we become! A hero to me is the one who can bring the truth to what one is at the time, and bring the good out of that person and others no matter what the circumstances of ones own life are. In fact, it is the circumstances that destroy or create ones character!

I was eventually transferred to the Ontario Training School for Boys in Colbourg. The training school was not easy to live at. It was like a military prison. We would march everywhere and there was no freedom they watched you all the time. I kept to myself and made no friends, I became an observer. I remember a boy named Jim Carr; he was from Yugoslavia who used to chew on his hand until it bled, but some how I was the same spirit as he was. He kept to himself and I was hurt to hear that he had died of pneumonia.

In the middle of the night some of the boys would slip down from their bunks and try to sexually harass me and I would defend myself. When the guard heard the noise they would make me stand in the hall until they thought I was tired enough to go to sleep, my back would ache. I have trouble with my back to this day. Once they had a new guard at the house, Mr. Robinson, who as we sat in our cubicles choked one kid out cold for no reason other than to scare us into behaving. I wanted to get away from the house and everyone. I wanted to be different than they were. I wanted to be away from them all. I wanted to be like Captain Nemo. To go on sick parade seemed like a way out. I went into the washroom. I felt very alone and lonely and missed my family. For the first time in my life I prayed, I prayed for a bleeding nose and hit myself and my nose began to pour blood, but the unusual thing was that the blood smelled like fish! For some reason, I recognized the fish was a symbol of God! I began to withdraw more and more into myself. I was lonely; there was nobody who loved me, nobody who cared!

One day, I found out that the kids who had flat feet wore brown shoes. I thought, here is one way I could be different. So, when I went to the doctor's and he asked me to stand on the floor and make an imprint to see if I had flat feet, when he wasn't looking I pushed down on my calf with my other foot. It worked, the doctor ordered brown shoes with arch supports. One would think that I would have learned discipline in the training school, but what I learned was to stay away from people. I got into a fight and the kid bit my finger, and deformed it, and every time I let someone into my space they hurt me! I stayed to myself and I didn't participate in sports or activities. I remember they used to give candies to the good kids, but I usually didn't get them before we marched to the movies on Saturdays. I remember the film Old Yeller and I cried when the dog was put down.

My Dad came and visited me in Colbourg, no body else did, I felt left behind. Afterwards, I began asking myself why was I there, what did I do wrong to be sent to a reform school? Was poverty a crime? I began to think of getting out of there. I began to think of a way to escape. They would march the kids down to a park in Colbourg and we would swim in Lake Ontario and when they would blow the whistle, you would have to hold your buddies hand up. I timed the whistles and after they took count and blew the whistle all clear, I had it planned with my buddy to escape. After the last whistle blew we dove under the water and under the roped off area and into where all the normal people were swimming. We swam and walked all day along the beach reaching Port Hope. We slept in a cardboard box we buried in the sand. We went into town cold and hungry and were looking for food and clothes when the police spotted us, picked us up and returned us to the training school. I was put in a jail cell. The thing that hurt me the most was that when they returned me to the house the other kids rejected me, for they lost privileges because of me running away. I became even more and more withdrawn and didn't participate in-group activities. I, like Captain Nemo, began to dislike people. There was a social worker named Mr. Cowan. He began to work with me to go home. I took a train trip home to the farm for Christmas one year.

I came to the farm a couple of times and remember when I was left alone I was devious and cruel! My second taste of the forbidden fruit was when I frolicked in the barn with a cousin. I shot a steel rod from a bow through a chicken and felt great remorse. I saw a snake in the chicken coop and made up a story that it was a copper-headed rattlesnake! Once you get a lie started it takes a lot of energy to keep it going because you have to remember the lie.

When I had returned to the reform school dad visited me. I was told he and my mom were there! Dad showed up with another woman and told me: this is your new mother. But, when I returned home again Dad was with my true mom, I said nothing. I was twelve years old when Mr. Cowan brought me home from the Reform School to stay. When my mother opened the door she was crying! I couldn't figure out why was she crying? I didn't understand. I thought she was crying because she was sad to see me! As I look back on it now, I realize she cried because of her great joy to see me. My mom truly loved me.

Now, my parents had moved from the farm and lived in an old house on what was called the mountain. It was maybe five miles from Midland, Ontario. I started to go to school at a one room schoolhouse. Life was not easy. There was not always a lot of food and my father was hard on me. I used to chop wood for the only source of heat and we cooked on an old wooden stove. I started to get in trouble at school. One kid was ringing the school bell and I told him if he rang it one more time I would hit him over the head with it. He did and I did. The school teacher gave me the strap in front of the class. I remember once Mr. Cowan came to visit us. My mom and him cooked up a plan to scare me into being good. He said he had heard bad reports about me and was there to take me back to the Training

School. I was quite ready to accept my fate. He asked me if I was going to be good? Of course I said yes! He decided to let me stay, for at least there I could be by myself.

But, being alone sometimes is not always good. I had heard that cats could land on their feet every time they fall. So I took a young cat we had and climbed a tree and dropped the cat. Each time I would go higher up the tree and drop the cat. I wasn't thinking of hurting the cat, I was just curious how high he could fall from and land on his feet. After, about four times the cat died! I was horrified and swore I would never kill anything else in my life. On the mountain, stones come to the surface and need to be picked up in the fields. My dad and I took a job picking stones and putting them on a cart. I was sitting on the edge of the wagon swinging my feet and my foot got caught under the wheel, the wagon full of stones ran over my body. My dad thought I would be dead. But, I got up and brushed my clothes off and carried on. I wasn't hurt at all, there must have been a guardian angel watching over me that day. My dad was amazed.

I have always been a thinker! I would often stare into space! My father would ask me, "What are you thinking about? Where do you go in thought?" I have always been in my own world. My problem was that I couldn't stop thinking! I discovered early, there was a fear within me! I remember once when a person began to ask me questions about myself. I began to shake, I was afraid to discover who I was! Why wouldn't I fear? Reality is, this is a scary place to be without God, without hope, without purpose, and not knowing where we come from, or where we are going.

The winters were cold and there was lots of snow. I hold in fond memories of dad when he would sharpen what he called the Swede saw and the axe. We would go out into the freezing cold weather and cut logs and chop wood and then carry the wood into the house and stack it by the wood stove. Before we could get out of the house dad used to light a fire under the motor of his old dodge to warm up the motor enough to get it started. Then, we had to shovel the driveway out and we no sooner got it shoveled out and the snowplow would fill it back in again. Which he would respond by some words I hadn't heard before! Then, dad and I used to drive into town and shovel the snow off of the roofs to make money. I seen him slide off the roof, get up, brushed himself off and went again.

My dad was strict with me. He would tell me if I cleaned the house he would give me five bucks to go into town. I would clean up and get myself duded up to go into town but when he came home he would say: "It is not clean enough" and he would make me do it again. I think he was a little jealous of me for some reason. I remember going to Little Lake Park on Firecracker night. Dad caught me at the park kissing a girl on a park bench, and he pulled me back and up over the bench. My dad was trying to keep me out of trouble. When we lived on the mountain when I was 14 years old, I used to climb to the top of the wooden ski jump and sit up there by myself. The height of that ski jump was over a hundred feet high. In the winter I went tobogganing at the ski hill. One guy was so mad at me for going down the hill that he hit me with a ski pole. I came home with welts on my body. Dad got so mad he went back with me to kick the guy's ass but he was nowhere to be found.

I remember our last Christmas Eve on the mountain. My father had not been working and our house was completely void of any signs of Christmas except for the Christmas songs on the radio. It certainly wasn't going to be the perfect

Norman Rockwell Christmas for us, but even still there were some child-like expectations within me. The spirit of Christmas hung in the air like an aroma, with the best yet to come! Unknown to me, my father, not content to let this be his fate for this Christmas Eve, decided to take a hike into town and try and scrounge up some kind of Christmas for us. Apparently, my dad hoofed all around town, and wasn't too lucky. So in his frustration, he decided to ask the guy at the drug store for credit, and came home to make a Christmas for us that was my most memorable. My father and mother didn't tell me anything, and when I went to bed I hung up one of my old grey socks, for no matter how poor we were, Santa Claus wouldn't forget me! My father didn't get a tree that year, but instead created a fireplace made out of cardboard boxes and red paper brick. Beneath the fireplace was an assortment of wrapped packages. As I unwrapped all of these little gifts, I found it strange that they where not the usual kind that Santa's helpers made, but the kind found in a drug store. It didn't take me long to figure out what my dad had done, but the joy on my parents' faces caused me to pause, not to question, and believe in Santa Claus one more time for them!

Once while waiting for my dad to come home from work, I heard his car door close, and then I heard it again, I thought we had a guest but when I looked out, there was no one there. I was hearing things! When we weren't busy trying to keep warm I would always listen to the rock and roll on the radio, music has always been a source of healing for me, I loved to sing. We had a black and white, one station CKVR television. My favorite program was Sea Hunt and I started a Fan club. I also remember one cold winter mom was very sick and would cough all the time. She was pregnant at the time! She would not go to the hospital. Dad and I helped to deliver another baby but the baby was dead on delivery. The cord had wrapped around the babies' neck no doubt from the persistent coughing.

We moved across the bay in Midland. We lived three miles from town. My parents were lead to believe they where buying the cottage but were only renting. We had to pump our water from a well. There was no bath; we had a wood stove that had to be fired up for cooking and hot water. I broke out with pimples all over my face. The basin mom used as a urine basin was the same basin I bathed in after mom would throw it out in the morning. I remember building my mom a shower out of an old five-gallon pail that I punched holes in the bottom and hung it from a tree, hung a curtain and poured water into the pail so my mom could take a shower. Through it all mother always had a sense of humor. My mother could have chosen to complain, but she chose to be grateful instead. Mom's attitude was that of being content in the moment. In all the things that happened to her she remained thankful. Because of mom's depression she often felt stressed and grew tired and retreated to her room. She isolated herself in her room. She began to put on a lot of weight. I don't want anyone to get the idea we were unhappy. We were just as happy as people who had more. My mother sought her joy in the things around her, the earthly beauty. Dad always found a way! I would have to say although they were poor they had a sense of holiness. I learned from poverty, I am glad I was born into poverty! It seemed to me in general the poorer the people were the more holy they were; evil increases the wealthier one becomes. I have heard it said: "Adversity creates men; prosperity creates monsters!" – Francis Hugo. They had their own value system, they were not carried along by the values of the middleclass. I seem to take on that same attitude! I learned that happiness is a state of mind and has nothing to do with what we have or even the circumstances in life. I have learned from my mother that acceptance is a big part of peace! Once one accepts one's weaknesses or circumstances, one can then begin to see or create beauty around oneself. Criticism is useless. Better to light a candle, than to curse the darkness!

I began to attend Midland Public School. My Mom and Dad were good to me and bought me new clothes to go to school. I dressed myself in black, and I dress in black to this day. I was put into a remedial class and met some friends. The three of us hung around, and called ourselves the white lightning gang. We had jean jackets with a white lighting streak on the back, and rode bicycles. It was the first time I had any friends. I got into the usual trouble and got the strap over the p.a. system as an example to the others for fighting on school grounds. Seems everywhere I went I had to defend myself. My friends would encourage me to fight the toughest guy in their circle of friends. And, after I fought him no one challenged me after that. I really appreciated being with those guys. One unusual occurrence took place when I was in Public School for reasons I do not know why but I spotted a beautiful Irish girl. She was an Anglican Minister's daughter. I fell in love with her! It was a pure innocent love; my heart would race when I saw her. It was a beautiful feeling. It was a spiritual love, something I have sought after all my life. It gave me hope! But, I knew she was out of my league. I would ride my bicycle home after school, and sometimes I would cut through the woods and I would stop and in the silence, I would feel a presence. Stephen was born there in that cottage and dad and I delivered him. I would have been 13 years old then. I remember holding Stephen, covered in blood, still not cleaned up by the stove fire, with amazement, and I questioned even more the meaning of life.

Each Sunday we would take a trip to the Refuge dump and ruffle through the garbage for anything of value, looking for items that dad could fix and sell. We always came home with more that we took. I built my own bicycles from spare parts. I remember one bicycle I put together out of spare parts and I painted it all white. I was proud of that bike. I remember my dad and mom getting into a fight because mom bought me streamers for the handlebars. Dad taught me practical things, to use tools, to fix things on my own, we had to fix everything ourselves because we could not afford to take things in to get fixed. He taught me many practical applications, which I later passed on to my son Darren. Dad also passed this mechanical ability to Stephen also. Everything I fixed had to be done perfect or he would make me do it again. Dad had a sense of compulsive disorder. He used to chew his tongue to the side when he was repeating things to perfection. This sense of perfectionism affected me later in my life.

I was transferred to Midland High School and to everyone's surprise I passed grade nine. I became active in track and field and began winning some of the events and was given a small trophy for Track and Field. I even had my picture in the local newspaper! A lawyer approached my mom and dad and asked them if he could sponsor me for the Olympics. But, when I returned to school the next year, they put me back into grade nine. My dad was angry and he ended up signing me out of school saying he needed me more at home to help support the family. I was fifteen.

I had some fun times of dad teaching me to drive his old car. It was a 1947 Dodge Sedan. He would let me drive at an early age and we would go for short trips to Wasaga Beach. Once I almost got into an accident, the old man would slap me on the head when I didn't pay attention to driving. The car was totally rusted, there was no floor, you could see the ground, the seats were held in place with two by fours of lumber and when we traveled down the dusty road we would come home all covered in white dust. The doors were wired together with coat hanger wire. The whole car was held together with wire. Every car we had was held together with coat hanger wire. Once on the way to Midland, the brakes failed, and the car was picking up speed going down a hill. My mother was trying to jump out, as I sat in that back seat I watch my dad react; his movements were like a choreographed dancer. He had one foot pumping the brakes, one hand on the steering wheel, and one hand on mom stopping her from jumping out, and one hand on the brake lever trying to stop the car with the emergency brakes, but as usual it didn't work either. I was always embarrassed to be seen in that car. Once on the way home the gas pedal fell off and dad hooked up a wire for a pull gas pedal. Another time the fuel pump was acting up and I had to get inside the motor with the hood up and pour gas into the carburetor, I learned how much to pour to go so fast. Dad eventually gave me that car, and I took it apart piece by piece and it is buried in the front yard of that cottage.

We moved into the town of Midland and my dad got a job working at the Midland Planning Mill, driving a lumber truck. My dad and I were increasingly at odds with each other. And, I wanted to run away. I packed my toothbrush and stole my dad's old pick-up truck and took off. Upon rounding a turn in the road I side swiped a van and took off, the cops started to chase me, and I hid the truck in a bush.

I walked home and dad was furious, I took him to where the truck was. He couldn't figure how I got the truck so far into the woods. I went to court; the police report was that they were chasing me at speeds up to 90 miles an hour. I was let off, and promised my dad I would owe him a truck. The next thing I knew I was accused of robbing the Beaver Lumber, but the shoe print did not match my shoes.

I remember one time my friends, Gary and Luke, and I were taking a couple of girls out in Port McNicholl. Once when we went with Gary's Father's car into the town to pick up the girls and a whole army of young men came running down over the hill to beat us up. Gary kicked at one guy and lost his shoe. I grabbed a tire iron out of the car and forced the gang leader to give Gary back his shoe. I started to hang around with a bad crowd, and was beginning to drink more and more. In those days we would go to barns, quarries, or the bush and have parties. I drank in the hotels for I looked older for my age. I got involved with a couple brothers who were always in jail. Once I went with these brothers to a barn party and when I was there the two brothers stole a cow and beat it to death with a tire iron. I wasn't involved but in the newspaper the next day was a story of cattle rustling.

When I turned sixteen, I took my dad's car for the road test. I began to unwire the door and the driving examiner thought I was nuts and refused to get into the car. One of my dad's friends at work loaned me his car for the test and I got my chauffeurs drivers license. I became a notorious driver; I had no fear in a vehicle. I would race back and forth from Penetang to Midland. It was a dangerous highway. I remember, long forgotten, a young girl from the York family who was killed on that highway. I got a fine for something;

I think it was when they caught me doing donuts down the main street. I paid the fine but lost the receipt. I was arrested and put in Barrie jail.

Later, I bought a 55 Chevy. I took it out to the bush and cut the top off with a hacksaw and made it into a convertible. Then I painted the entire inside with red paint. I took my mom for a ride. We had a flat tire, and I didn't have money to fix it so I drove it with a flat with the sparks flying off the rim. I almost made it home until the cops tracked the rim marks to a block within my home. My poor mom got out of the car and her entire back was covered in red paint. They impounded the car, and we walked home.

My dad was concerned about my increasingly deviant behavior. I seemed to be drawn to the worst characters. And my dad and I were not getting along. Dad was getting more and more frustrated with me. I don't blame him. He expected me to pay my own way, but I couldn't hold the jobs in the factory. Mom did her best to look after Stephen who would have been three at the time. But, she was sick and stayed in bed and couldn't clean. Dad was working so he couldn't do it, but he tried. But, our home was dirty and unkept. I wouldn't clean either; I just thought it was normal. Dad would give me a few dollars for cleaning up sometimes. Most of the time there wasn't clean clothes, face soap or toothpaste. But, my mom tried, I remember my mom using an old ringer washer. One night I remember I was awakened by something crawling on me. I called to dad and found in the crevices of the mattress were maggots. Dad just flipped the mattress over and I told me to go back to sleep. Almost every place we moved from was condemned. I hated those fly stickers that hung from the ceiling. They would stick to the side of my face and the flies would buzz in my ear. My mom had cats and they would crap all over and smell.

Dad would get frustrated with the cats under his feet and one day as I was coming down the side walk, I saw the cats flying right through the front door screen. It was funny, but when dad kicked my dog, that was a different thing and we got into a fight. I wasn't a kid anymore! I pushed him down on the floor and almost pasted a milk glass bottle into his face. My dad could have literally killed me after all he was a soldier but dad did nothing. When I looked into his eyes, I was hurt and he was hurt. I respected him. Yet I knew it was time for change!

We moved a couple of times and I got a job working in a couple of factories and became ill, I felt claustrophobic. I saw the people work hard all their lives, fought and killed to obtain materialism and it only decays in the end! It didn't seem worthwhile to spend my whole life in search of materialism. I continued to get together with my friends. One time, we bought a bottle of bootlegged Zing and went to a dance in Penetang. When I heard the band I was mesmerized. I wanted to do that! I lost all interest in chasing the girls that night. I listened to music it fed me spiritually, and gave me hope and a dream for the future and I realized I was destined for something different than the night shift.

I was a handsome young man and the women in Midland were attracted to me. But, what did I know about love, my heart was hard. I could have treated them better. I remember my first real sexual experience when I was sixteen in the back of Gary's father's car parked at the Plastic Factory where he worked the night shift. In those days they didn't lock the cars. Her name was Dianne. Later, I decided to break up with her and told her at a movie theater. I remember the movie was starring Cliff Richard in "Bachelor Boy". When I told her she pulled out a cutting knife she had from working at the plastic factory and wanted to kill herself! I grabbed the knife off her and tossed it to Gary a couple of seats back and he threw it back to her. Gary was beginning to date a girl from Toronto and I on occasion went with her girlfriend, Beverley. My uncle Mac took me to a stock car race; and I was so impressed I wanted to become a racecar driver. I built a stock car and named it Bev but I never got the thing out of the back yard and didn't hear from Bev again either. I remember writing a pen pal letter to a girl in Liverpool England. How I got her address I don't remember. When she wrote me she asked me if I had a Beatle haircut. All my friends got jobs and began to settle in but I couldn't do it. Not long after that I was to leave Midland. Later, Gary and Luke were married and divorced and Luke's wife died of cancer. My favorite song playing on the radio at that time was "Raindrops" by Dee Clark.

This was my early years and the end of my youth and innocence that would have an influence on me for the rest of my life. In a way, I was socially crippled. I was born into a counter cultural family, an outcast, lost and in search of my own individuality. In my youth I had the desire to race cars, sing and play music. More than this, my childhood had imbedded in me a desire to fight for my mom and dad. They were the symbol of the lost and the forgotten, and in that I would find my purpose.

CHAPTER TWO

"Escape to St. Catharines"

MY MOM USED to give me a few dollars when she could and I would go down to Little Lake Park in Midland. The park was a hang out of mine. I would go for a swim or rent a rowboat or buy a few fries. I was always hungry. There wasn't a lot of food in our house! We never had a mealtime. Dad would bring groceries home and they would be gone in a short period of time. On my way home from the Park I would always walk by the minister's daughter's house in hope that I might see her! I never saw her again; funny. I never even talked to her! Yet, I felt a beautiful innocent love in my heart for her, I believe now what I recognized was the spirit of Jesus dwelling within her! I pray she kept her innocence!

My life was about to change when I was at Little Lake Park; I met a family, a mother and her two daughters. They invited me back to their campsite. When, after they asked me what I was doing with my life they ask me if I wanted to go to St. Catharines with them? I thought since my Dad and I weren't getting along and I wasn't going anywhere with my life, I said I would go with them. I returned home said "Goodbye" to my mom. I felt bad for leaving her. I picked up my toothbrush, and returned to the campsite and I left with them to go to St. Catharines. They treated me very well. They took me to Markarian's Sub Shop by the Welland Canal and Port Weller. I never tasted a sub before and I wolfed it down and they bought me another one. Pat showed me around St. Catharines. We eventually parted company and I moved into a boarding home and began working picking peaches. I never saw them again and I never had the chance to say thanks. My next job was as a bouncer at a tavern. The drinking age was twenty-one back then. They didn't know I was only seventeen. I looked older than I was. I eventually got a job working at a factory grinding metal hydro boxes. I met a couple of brothers who were sharing a house and they asked me to move in with them. Things were going well. I just appreciated having a bath everyday and clean clothes and my pimples disappeared. Those guys always had women around but I wasn't that interested! Although it was the time of free love I had it in my heart to find the kind of innocent love I experienced before! It wasn't so much the women as it was the kind of love I was searching for. Not to long after I was living in the house the guys went to a CYO Catholic Dance. Marlene and her girl friend were invited back to our house by one of the guys who had a crush on her. Marlene didn't have an interest in the fellow and we began to talk and she gave me her telephone number. And, we began to talk on a regular basis. I thought when I met her that since she looked young she would be good to marry because she would look young when she was old. I eventually lost my job and took a room in what was known as the City House. I had a hard time fitting in and holding jobs and was on the move, having a number of different jobs and living in a number of different places. Marlene and I continued to date each other and after six months, she told me she was pregnant. The most honorable thing to do was to marry. Marlene's uncle Arnold provided a 1957 Black Cadillac and we got married in a small Immaculate Conception Roman Catholic Church, on Church Street in St. Catharines on December 31, 1965. I agreed with the Priest to raise my kids Catholic and I sent them to Catholic Schools. We were both eighteen years old. Neither one of us were prepared for marriage.

I got a job working in a paper mill and we moved into an apartment across from the Paper Mill. Marlene's grandmother signed for us for new furniture from the Bad Boy Store. As hard as I tried I couldn't hold down a job in that factory, I felt closed in. I hated it. Marlene and I were at each other's throats, we were fighting all the time. We had hard times, we couldn't afford to live, we had our furniture re-possessed and after Darren was born he came home from the hospital, he slept in a baby buggy. I took a job as a truck driver in a laundry company. Marlene spent her time looking after Darren. Marlene had Darren when she was 19 years old. I was 18.

I was constantly thinking, I needed answers; I needed to know who I was! Where did I come from, why was I here and where was I going after this short time on earth? These questions seemed most important to me. It seemed pointless to me to spend my life in search of materialism. Marlene's father, Marcel, even got me a job working at his factory but I got fired when I knocked over a pile of furnaces. I felt very depressed and disappointed in myself because I had let them down and I let myself down! I was carrying a lot of baggage and issues from my past. I was angry, everyone had rejected me, and I had no support from anyone. All the time I was in the Children's Aide, no one came to visit me. The whole Goodnough family disowned me. My brothers and sisters, all of my family were gone! I was left to defend for myself. I also, had an inward fear that my family too was going to be taken from me by the smart talking social workers that had taken me away from my family and put me into the Training School for Boys.

I couldn't fit in! I couldn't help it; I was a failure at everything. I had been drinking since I was 14 years old. And, as the stress increased I began drinking all the more. I got into the wrong crowd again and I was unfaithful to Marlene. I didn't know what love was! Who loved me, that I should know love! I was insensitive to anyone's feelings at that time. I couldn't tell her. I was now carrying guilt and I hated and loathed myself. I began to hate everyone. I was depressed and felt anxious all the time, and drank to curb my fear. I went to see Dr. Coholon and he asked me if I had been unfaithful? He prescribed anti-depressant pills. These pills made me worse and created more anxiety in me, and I stopped taking them and continued to drink. The drink became both my friend and my enemy. I couldn't shut my mind off. Beer for me was a way to shut my brain off.

I started searching for my brothers Brent, Ted, and Richard and my sister Lana hoping I could regain my family. I was an empty vessel. I was a lost soul. I find it strange that I couldn't remember being around or seeing or playing with my family. It has seemed to me I was an only child. Brent was born in Oshawa, but I can't remember Brent, Ted or Lana! It was my mom who, years later, told me about the rest of my family. After much communication with the

Children's Aide Society I found my brothers Brent and Ted, and had a couple of visits with my sister Lana. I was able to bring them home to see mom. But, I realized we could only be a family by name because we had grown up apart. Ted blamed me for not coming and taking him out of there. At one point I did go and kidnap Ted and take him out of where he was. I took him to live with us in St. Catharines; but he complained that we only had Kraft dinner to eat and decided to return to Browndale.

I made regular trips to see my mother and father in Midland. I didn't really want to sleep over for it wasn't clean and I felt dad was disappointed in me as well. Perhaps he felt I had abandoned them! And, in our hard times we were forced to go live with them in a crowded shack in the country. The walls were thin there was no privacy. My dad and I didn't get along and often fought over me not taking the bucket of crap out and dumping it. In desperation, I made an application to join the Armed Forces. One had to be single to join. I lied and told them I wasn't married. Marlene returned to St. Catharines to live with her parents and I was posted in Edmonton. I was so lonely and lost without Marlene and Darren. I got drunk with the recruits and slept with a native woman. After a couple of months the Army discovered I was married. I was sent to a detention jail for ten days and after my time was up, I was given an honorable discharge and sent home to St. Catharines.

I was so glad to see Marlene and Darren. It meant a lot to me to be going to what I began to call home with Marlene and her family; I began to think of them as my family. It has been my honor and perhaps my salvation to share in her families' life in the good and the bad, the deaths and mourning. They are the closest thing I ever had to a normal family. When I came home from the Army

I really wanted to do good. I took a course on how to operate heavy equipment and got a job driving scrapers on the Welland Canal Project. We couldn't work all the time because of the rain. On the off-season we would collect unemployment insurance. One day an unemployment officer came to my apartment and told me I had frauded the government, by collecting unemployment insurance payments when I was working! Which was untrue. I didn't sign those unemployment cards! I have an idea who it was but thought it would be honorable for me to take this upon myself. The Unemployment officer was at the door and were threatening me to go to court for fraud and jail. Marlene and I panicked and went on the move, and hid from the cops and began a transient lifestyle. I was a lost soul; I just couldn't get it together, or fit in.

Our lifestyle was in poverty. We lived off of the food banks. I didn't know what was going to happen to us next but I felt safer when we kept moving around! I was my own worst enemy. We fought, drank, and smoked some pot, which made me more paranoid. The herb is likened to the fruit in the Garden of Eden. The fruit of the knowledge of Good and Evil! I became paranoid because I was afraid of the knowledge of who I was!

I was lost and I knew it! But, I was to become even more lost. Once, we were given a love drug called MDA by a supposed friend. It might have been LSD I'm not sure. This proved to be a most frightening life changing experience. No one seems to know what happened to me. Marlene can't recall it. Days were just lost! The only thing I remember after we took the drug was a dog growling at me. The rest is blank. All I know is that I opened the door for evil to come into me. I entered into an altered state, a place of evil. This altered state would return to me, time after time, year after year. I really had a hard time with it, for it kept returning. My ears rang all the time. It wasn't the seen world that frightened me; it was the unknown realm that frightened me! I lived in fear, for any situation would bring it on. I was with relatives, the first time this altered state return to me! I didn't return to that relative because I was afraid it would come back on me again. I sat on the side of a canal bank, saying to myself, I can't live like this, and if this didn't stop I didn't want to live on. I became afraid to be in situations I couldn't control, planes, bridges, elevators, and high-rise buildings. I became paralyzed by fear. I was afraid to get on a bus, was afraid to get close to any heights; I didn't trust myself. I was constantly thinking. I became sensitive about everything. At first I tried to run away from myself, afraid to face it The battle was within myself! I separated myself from others and the only time I could be at peace and stop thinking and live in the moment was when I was drinking. In the past, I have been too afraid to face it, and I didn't want to worry my family. All of my life I have lived in fear; afraid to live and afraid to die!! My life had become a continuous daily struggle. Some days I eat the bear; but sometimes the bear would eat me! Tired of being pre-occupied and living a life of fear; I tried fighting my fear and challenged myself. I began to push myself beyond safe! I took up scuba diving, motorcycling, dirt biking, and fast cars. But these fears were to remain with me for most of my life. I have never touched any drugs since, not even an aspirin to this very day.

It was a time of change. John F. Kennedy, who although was shot when I was in school a few years before; left a valor lingering in the air. It was a time of Woodstock and traveling, and the sweetest music and lyrics filled the air. *"I came upon a child of God he was walking along the road, and I asked him where he was going. This he told me, I'm going to camp out on the land and join a rock n roll band, Cause we have to get ourselves back to the Garden!"* It seemed the world was traveling, in VW mini vans, and school buses, and anything that moved. Seeking purpose, it was calling us to abandon materialism and find ourselves. I wanted to be part of it! Vancouver seem to be the place to be where things where happening! It became a lifestyle for us to sell everything and take off on the train to Vancouver. I was in search of myself. Marlene didn't see it as a search for meaning but a burden of poverty. Marlene was rightly concerned about security. Darren would sleep in a drawer. And, through the years Darren attended 75 different schools. Once, Marlene found a two-dollar bill under a bridge. You would have thought we found a million dollars. But no matter where you go you take yourself with you and I lived in a constant state of fear and hell. When people would question me about myself I would shake with fear for I was afraid of who I was!

Upon returning home to St.Catharines it wasn't very long before I started to feel restless and feeling the world closing in on me again; we sold all we had and traveled to Vancouver another time where I met "Old Earl", as he was affectionately called. He was to this explorer, just another old man living in a run down welfare St. Francis hotel in Vancouver. It was a place where everyone there was a transient. I assumed by the way that he was dressed that he was just another old person discarded by society. I became curious about him and I soon changed my mind about him. I was told that Earl lived there permanently. He was unusual; he was special, helpful and kind. He was not bitter or influenced by those around him; instead he spent his time talking and encouraging the lonely and lost people around him. I was curious as to why? I discovered that he had been a missionary in the Philippines and worked with prisoners who where condemned to be executed. It was there that he had contacted malaria, which is how he lost his sight. Upon returning to Canada the church gave him a small pension and wanted him to retire but he wanted no part of that. I don't think he was ever married instead he gave his all for God! He cared less about recognition from this world; for he was not judged by this world! It was from him that this young man first heard the story of another homeless person who lived years ago, whose name was Jesus! I know by now Earl must be with the Lord and I am sure that there would not have been much of a worldly salute to Earl but after all these years I remember him and my tribute to him is that now I tell the story of the homeless Jesus, also! I befriended him as well as two other people there. The one fellow was just a boy at the time. The other was a man from Newfoundland called Scuby. The old man had befriended him and was convincing him to return to Newfoundland and face up to the trouble he had caused. I remember he stole a boat and the police where after him. I didn't tell Earl my own problem with the law. I connected with the young fellow who was just learning to play his guitar. I had bought an old classical guitar for $20.00 from a pawnshop and was teaching myself how to play it. The three of us became good friends and when I found an apartment I used to have them over for supper but moved and continued my journey!

Once I was walking down the street in Vancouver, I heard a voice above my head. He said to me: "Larry I am here"! I answered by saying, "Lord, I know you're here; but I have no proof of you!" I didn't even trust myself anymore. I didn't forget that voice though. I went to a doctor's office once to ask the doctor why my ears rang all the time. The ringing became so loud at times it was driving me nuts. This constant ringing was like the sound I used to hear from the hydro lines while walking down the country roads in my youth. I'm not sure where that sound comes from; it is the sound of a loud hissing sound, like that of a snake hissing. The doctor told me it came from excessive noise damage perhaps, from the sound of the heavy equipment I worked on and there was nothing he could do for me. That day and with the voice of Jesus fresh still in my mind; I called out to Jesus: "Jesus if you are real, stop this ringing in my ears"! Later in the day, I noticed the ringing was gone! To this day the ringing still comes back, but, each time it comes back, I say: "Satan, be gone and stop hissing in my ears, in Jesus name"! And it is gone again! I fought to get control of myself. I was now afraid to take any drugs, and I knew if I reached out for help from the doctors they would give me drugs. Once, I dropped into a Christian coffee shop and a Christian family took us in and showed us Christian love, it meant a lot to me. It was one of those steps along the way. The Graham family's kindness left a positive impression on us of what Christian love was meant to be.

They helped us and we returned to St. Catharines once more. But this time life was beginning to get better and we were more lucky than usual! We lucked out and got a cottage right on the water. I met a man who ran a driving school and I applied for a driving instructor's license, and began to give high school teenagers driving lessons. After that I decided to begin a driving school of my own and managed to get a loan, got a car and began to teach.

Then luck began to go sour again when the bill collectors saw my name on the driving school sign and followed me home! I knew it was only going to be a matter of time before the police would be at my door. The driving instruction and the pressure of bill collectors and Marlene was now pregnant with Tara stressed me out and I began to experience social anxiety and panic disorder and I had to stop teaching. It was there in that cottage that one morning while lying in bed I heard a voice for the second time. This time a voice said in an evil deep voice, "I am going to get you!" Trying to relieve stress I decided to give myself up! I told Marlene I was going to give myself up and get this over with. I took the bus downtown and gave myself up to the police. On my way to the bus, a cat cornered a bird and the bird was chirping for his life. Strange it bothered me that I should feel bad for not helping that bird. God's spirit was beginning to work on me that I should feel for a bird! When I gave myself up. I was put in a cell and later I was sentenced to three months in jail. Tara was born when I was in jail. Marlene was 26 years old. Marlene brought Tara to the jail for me to see her for the first time.

When I was in jail, I kept to myself. For no reason a Guard came up to me and said: "you don't really care for anyone do you"! My response to him was: "you're wrong! I really do care; that is my problem!" The Guard felt he had misjudged me and told me to read a book called Nostradamus. That guard took a liking to me and gave me a jail cell of my own. Alone in my cell I kept thinking about what the future held for me. I thought about what the Guard had said and I came to an understanding of myself. I didn't really hate people; I really did love people. In fact what I needed more than anything in the world was to be loved and be accepted. I thought how love and hate were closely related to each other; they are both strong emotions. Three months later I was back home. It was sort of a beginning for me in a way for now I was beginning to face and understand myself. That was the last time I got in trouble with the law.

I was always concerned about my parents. After my mom was transported to a hospital in Toronto from Midland with pneumonia and almost died, I convinced my parents to move to St. Catharines. They moved, but wherever they lived, on Martindale Road where the Fire Department now is and off of Hartzel Road where Kentucky Fried Chicken is now, both were condemned and torn down! Off Hartzel Road they had a dog named Peter, he was a sort of bulldog and pit bull. We all laughed when once the mailman sprayed Peter and the dog took off after him and came home with the mailman's pants in his mouth. Another time I remember, it was around the time that Lana came to visit my mom, only one time! I was away when she came. That was the last anyone heard of her. Later I was to learn that Lana was supposed to have committed suicide by jumping into the Niagara Falls. Her body was never found. I often surmised that she was still alive and living another life! Ted also came to see mom. I had been away when they came. Before I left on another trip my dog Ipon was hit by a car and his back hip was broken. I had brought back that dog from out west and loved that dog. The veterinarian wanted five hundred dollars to fix him! Mom who didn't believe in doctors told me to leave him with her. I remember that Anne broke the cat's tail by slamming the car door on the cat. Mom patched up the cats tail by tape and sticks and when the cats tail was healed it had a bend in the tail and every time the cat would wag its tail it would spin like a windmill! I came home six months later and was so glad to see the dog running around the back yard as good as new!

Because I had owned the driving school I was able to buy two old houses, one for my parents. I lost my house when I couldn't keep the payments up. Dad and Mom raised Stephen and Anne there in that house. Mom was happy to be in St. Catharines. I remember once they had a Volkswagen van at Martindale. It broke down on a trip to Midland and I had to go and tow them back with a chain. I doubt if you could do that legally these days. My mom was afraid to be towed over the Skyway but I towed the van over the skyway. I could have pulled them under the Skyway but I didn't! Later in my life I became afraid of bridges and understood her fear! And later in life I also came to understand why she lived a life of solitude! Mom loved to go to the country, especially she liked Lakeshore Road were she could see the fruit stands and taste the peaches and grapes. But it was hard on her mentally, for when she returned she would relive each conversation. Mom was well most of the time. She had a beautiful humble spirit of God living within her! Marlene and her family said my mother was a saint! My mother taught me to have a sense of humor. She had nothing, she was laughed upon because of her size, and they laughed and scorned her, as Jesus, yet she was full of love and humor. She wore sunglasses in the house. She stayed in her bedroom, and when she ate chocolates she would take a bite out of each one of them so the kids wouldn't eat all of them on her. Mom had become much bolder; she used to make fun of my father who wasn't as witty as mom was. And, she used to loose patience with him. Dad would try to be wittier than her. I remember once him saying to her, be more pacific, mom's response was "pacific is the ocean"; my mom would say it is specific, in joking. And, when he seems to ask nonsense questions, she would say: "oh, just ask it!"

We spent a lot of time at my dad's place; we visited every other day. We spent good times in the backyard over a fire. When we had a party we used to drink to make us happy but Mom was happy within her own self and would laugh at us characters. One memory I will never forget was when I got drunk. Meaning well, they put me in my car and left it running to keep me warm. Then someone woke me up and I struggled upstairs and passed out in one of the kid's beds. When I woke up half poisoned by carbon dioxide I had a weird feeling between my buttocks, I was afraid to look! I had a big wad of bubble gum stuck between my cheeks!

My mother always called me the prodigal son. My mother didn't know how right she was! When I was to go on another journey my mom didn't want us to leave, she was always concerned for Stephen and Anne and tried to convince me to stay. She was worried that dad might hurt them! I was able to spend some time with Stephen scuba diving and dirt biking. I have good memories when dad and I began to scuba dive together. Mom would get mad at dad for melting old batteries down to make weight belts to sell to make a few bucks. Money was always tight but mom loved to go to the A&W Drive In. Once Marlene and I went with them to the drive in and Anne was sitting on my mom's lap sipping a large iced cola when Anne spilled the drink down my mom's top and my mom let out a scream: "Christ, right up my ass!" Marlene and I slid down into the back seat as not to be seen! Mom rarely left the house but once, Marlene and my mom went to a shoe store and mom spent her baby bonus and bought new shoes. When she came home dad, being so used to her buying from second hand stores, said to her they look brand new! They were brand new! He gave her heck for spending the money on new shoes. The last memory I have of her was I used to go to the house to work on my van. I was rebuilding the inside into a camper. Mom was sick, I felt she was faking most of the time. She had an electric blanket on her to keep warm. I convinced her to unplug the blanket so I could use the power drill to fix my van. She told me, you don't realize how sick I am!

That night I got up at around 3:00 a.m. as usual in the nude and was sitting at the table eating some cereal. I felt someone was watching me. I looked around thinking perhaps the kids got up! But, there was nobody there! In the morning my dad came over to tell me that my mom had died in her sleep. Probably at the same time I was up, perhaps she came to see me once more before she left. My dad couldn't handle it well and ask me if I would come over and help him and make arrangements for the funeral. We had to go to the Welfare Office and argue with Mr. Nabbie, the caseworker, for he wasn't happy that mom needed an oversize coffin. Inwardly, I felt bad about unplugging her heating blanket to fix my van. I lost my desire for the van and sold it shortly after. I wish I had not been so selfish! I wished I had been more sensitive and spent more time with her. I wished I had gotten her an old piano to play. But, one good thing I did was to bring all of her children home for her to see before she died. All the teenagers in the area loved my mom and came to her funeral. I tried to show no emotions! I held it all in until they lowered her into the grave and I couldn't hold back any more and broke down and cried probably the first time in a long time. When I think of her death, it still brings a pain in my heart and a tear to my eye. I tried to hold my feelings in for years. I just didn't want to face it! But I had not fully grieved my mom. One day I was drinking with a buddy I went to college with, when all of a sudden I started to cry and I excused myself. On the way home I pulled off the road and just sobbed. I drove down to the graveyard at 2:00 a.m. in the morning and got out but I couldn't find her grave; we couldn't afford a stone for her grave. I looked around and came to my senses and said: "what the hell am I doing in this graveyard?" I took off glad to be out of there. I wish I had spent more time with both my parents. I loved them both. My mom had her own joy within herself. I used to question her faith, but she would just say: "you will see!" I was lost in those days. I just couldn't see, I was blind, I regret my blindness and selfishness, and I wish I had done more, loved more.

What I remember was the laughter, the funny things. My dad had a British nose with a little knob on the end. Mom used to call him Becker. I remember that each time my palm would itch she would say you're going to come into some money. Mom was a character on her own. I prefer to remember her sense of humor and her humble character.

Once when I lived on Elma Street in St. Catharines, we had no food and so I went to the church behind our house and begged for food. They said they don't do that. So I went to the other smaller church behind us also, and they came and gave us groceries and vegetables from their gardens. A short time later a paving company came in and began to pave the church that refused us food but could afford pavement? One night, I got drinking and it bothered me. So, I got a bucket of red paint and went out to the new pavement and painted: "GOD MAY FORGIVE YOU FOR THE TAR BUT WILL THE STARVING CHILDREN OF THE WORLD?" Then it started to rain and thunder and the whole sky was lighting up, I thought God was angry and he was going to get me so. I signed the bottom with a CROSS and took off running for the door! This reminds me of a Martin Luther moment.

A while later a young man came to my door and asked me: "Did I know Jesus and where I was going after I died?" He was a newly placed Emmanuel Bible College graduate and was just assigned to the church in behind! The church I thought didn't live up to what they preached! So, I said, like the spider and the fly: "come on in!" I don't even smoke, but I blew smoke in his eyes. Then I said I am the one who painted your church! He, in his innocence, thought I meant I did some work painting for the church! I said, "No. I am the one who painted your church!" Archie came and visited me a couple of times and did convince me I needed to come to the Lord. One night by myself, I knelt before the Lord and asked for forgiveness and asked Jesus into my heart. But, really I didn't think the Lord could do anything with me! I thought I was beyond saving. And, let it go!

We moved into a new apartment. Archie followed me and preached to me a couple times. I was a lost human being at this time in my life and I knew it. I thought there was no hope for me. I had reverted to drinking hard liquor during the night and sleeping all day. We didn't have cable so we put up a homemade aerial with two wires. Drunk and moving side to side with the aerial I watched the programs. At that time the series Roots was on. I particularly remember the man was going back to Africa to find his roots! When the man told his girlfriend, she told him: "Well sometimes people need to loose themselves in order to find themselves." The man asked who said that? She said: Jesus said that! I knew I was lost and that hit home.

Interestingly, I watched a sermon one late night on the 700 Club. Ben Kinslow was talking about the prodigal son and being lost. I was lost! That night I got down in front of that TV and I prayed again! I prayed for forgiveness and to accept Jesus into my heart. I was thirty years old. (Interestingly, I live within a block of both of those places this day.) The next day I felt good, I felt I did something important. I felt I had a new beginning.

CHAPTER THREE

"Sing to the Lord a New Song"

I FELT I should tell Marlene about how I had called on the Lord and asked him to come into my life. She had already been through a lot and this was too much for her! Marlene and I separated for the first time! We had been married twelve years. She went and stayed with her parents and then she got an apartment in Port Dalhousie. I was now feeling very alone and depressed! It was at that time I began putting weight on!

I bought a bible, and I began reading the Old Testament. I earnestly prayed, Lord what would you want me to do? Lord? And, I cut the bible open to this passage Psalm 96: 1-3

> *Sing to the LORD a new song; Sing to the LORD, all the earth.*
> *Sing to the LORD, praise his name; proclaim his salvation day after day.*

Declare his glory among the nations, His marvelous deeds among all peoples."

This is an interesting passage for it spoke directly to me! Throughout my life I kept returning to this passage; for I believed God had spoken to me! The only ambition I harbored within myself at the time was that I wanted to sing and play my guitar. I began to read the bible in little bits. I felt God was speaking to me and encouraging me. "Rise from you slumber and God will shine on you!" But other times the Bible was like a battle, I got so tired reading and I would fall asleep. I began to loose heart again and I began thinking I was too far gone and God didn't want me. I took the bible back for a refund to buy some beer. Try to explain why you are taking a bible back for a refund!

Marlene and I started talking again and I moved in with her in Port Dalhousie, but once again we fought and she moved out! I started going to the bar in Port Dalhousie, degrading myself looking for sex, One time at the end of the night, a bartender told me you look lost, you need Jesus or something. I told her: "I tried that it doesn't work for me!"! That night I went out to my car, thinking of raising some hell. The streets were deserted and silent! As I leaned over to start my car, I heard a voice from my left side, it was the voice of an angel, a male and by the sound of his voice he would be around thirty years old! He said: "Go home Larry and call it a day!" I went home, and when I arrived home it was like somebody picked me up and threw me on the floor. I was terrified! I could barely stand! When we come to the day when we meet our Lord, if there is anything false about us it will melt away. We need to be able to stand before the Lord. When I woke up the next morning something had happened to me! I started reading the bible again, the Old

Testament. I threw out all my playboy magazines, I began to speak in a strange tongue, and I went over to my table and tried to write it down. Interestingly, I remember a story that my father told me about his father who was illiterate, but who wrote in beautiful scrolls of calligraphy after coming to the Lord! I went over to my window and stood their playing my guitar singing Amazing Grace and the tears were just streaming down my checks. I believe it was then that I was born again! When I went outside, the day was brighter; I felt I was saved to eternal life. As I was driving I saw a butterfly, and I saw the connection, like a butterfly I was born anew, I was transformed. For the first time I began to see clearly. My stomach was in my mouth; I had the fear of the Lord. Oh how I wanted to live a Godly life and be free from all guilt and fear. This was a holy healthy fear! It was like a compass was put within my heart, whenever I would stray off the path, the Spirit convicted me. I was afraid to do anything wrong! "Fear of the Lord is the beginning of wisdom."(Psalm 111:10) What was so incredible was I had this feeling of love and thanksgiving within me towards everything, the beauty of our world, the animals and especially for the lost sinner. The Spirit of God had opened the veil of my heart. I knew I was a creature of the knowledge of good and evil, original innocence and original sin! I was convinced that Jesus was the way! He paid the price for my sin, my guilt was gone! "He, who has been forgiven much; loves much!" I have heard it said: "I have a mantle of love over me!" Which has not left me to this day! And, that was the last time I ever heard voices again! The year was 1977 and I was 30 years old. Praise you Lord. Thank you Lord. You cared for me and didn't give up on me.

I was given the gift of faith; from that moment on my faith was sure, never to waver again. It was for me the beginning of my committed faith journey with God. My mind was and to this day is always on the Lord. I hunger for God. I couldn't think of anything else, doing what was right and serving God was all that mattered to me. I just wanted to be alone with God. I lost all interest in the things of the world. My heart became soft and I welled up at the stories of a savior who could save a sinner like me! I was twice blessed when I listened to Christian music, and I began learning to play Christian songs.

I made another effort to get back with Marlene. We both wanted to make a whole new start and decided to go to the United States. The money ran out and I ended up painting a motel for a place to stay on the beaches of Florida. Each morning I would face the east and pray to God as the sun came up. I started reading the Bible from Genesis. It was a strange time. I met a stranger on the shore. It has been a long time since I met him but his memory is as fresh in my mind as if it had happened yesterday! I was thirty-one, and it was the year when I had first become a Christian. I wanted to start a new life! I decided to sell everything we owned and move to a new city. And so, my wife, my daughter, my son, and myself sold everything we had and we traveled to Florida! My dreams of success soon fizzled out when the money ran out! Now it became a day-to-day survival! I was tempted to steal, so much wealth around me! This was my time of temptation in the desert! I instinctively knew that what I choose would set the course of the rest of my life! We where living in an old run down motel on the oceanfront. I had talked to the motel owner about our situation and he let me paint the motel for our daily stay! I used to get up every morning and go down to the beach and sit in amazement and meditate towards the sun, as it would rise from the east, and then paint the motel and scrounge for food the rest of the day!

One night, I was totally frustrated. What I was going to do with my life? How was I going to care for my family or for that matter get them home? I spent my last bit of money we had and I bought a six-pack of beer and I walked along the beach. There is something mysterious about the water at night! As I walked kicking sand I looked up to see someone in the fog and darkness. I saw a figure walking towards me. As I focused I realized it was a slim man with long hair. He seemed out of place! This stranger walked up to me, lifted his hand to me and rolled open his hand to reveal a beautiful, blue, florescent, pulsating, blue stone. We began to talk and almost immediately our conversation turned to religion as if it was the natural thing to talk about. I invited him back to my motel room where the conversation continued. He told us he had just become a Buddhist a year before and I told him I had just became a Christian a short while back myself. He said he was from Ottawa, Canada but for some reason it didn't settle with me! He didn't drink! To me, there wasn't a Canadian who didn't drink! We talked for quite a while and in the end he gave me the pulsating stone, and I put it in a jar and into my duffle bag. We talked into the night and then I walked the stranger back down to the beach and watched him disappear into the darkness and fog in the same way he appeared! When I returned to Canada I discovered that the jar was missing and for the life of me I can't remember his name or for that matter even the conversation! All I can remember about the stranger was the strange way he came and went. I am not sure of, or if there was any purpose to this meeting. He seemed to question my faith more than tell me of his own. Perhaps, he was interested in what I believed. Perhaps, he wasn't from

Canada at all! Perhaps, he wasn't a Buddhist! Perhaps, I met more than a stranger on the shore! And, oh how I wished I had made a better impression!

It was a couple of days before Christmas. I went to the Canadian Embassy and lucked out and got some bus ticket to go home! We returned to Canada broke and with scabies. I was different, I watched a beggar on Christmas day being thrown out of a bus station and my heart was hurting for him. We came home broke and begging. I had no idea where we were going to stay but Clem and Debbie, bless them, they took us in without question. It was Christmas and all were drinking. I drank too much and they all thought that would be the last they saw of me that night. I went behind to the side of the house fell over on my face and prayed, Lord, help me, and I got right back up sober! Thanks be to God I kept my respect!

I began to understand that my calling was for all those poor people I had seen on the streets and in food banks and welfare hotels. I fell in love with the homeless son who lived many years ago, and still lives today. I felt compelled to tell others about the love of God. I literally feel in love with God. Does one fall in love with someone who doesn't exist? I had made a choice; I turned my back on the material world. I vowed I would spend the rest of my life in search of God, and becoming an instrument of good. I began soaking up the scriptures and everything I could learn about Jesus. I attended many fundamental type churches listening to every speaker I could. I soon discovered that it was going to be a difficult task to do good in this world and a difficult task to find a place to belong. At first nobody even believed me. I was the prodigal son returning to the Father, and as in the story, the older son, (the church) treated me the same as in the story. They thought they were more deserving than I to receive the Father's love.

We grew restless and still hoping for a new beginning decided to try out west. I had an old 1964 Green Chrysler totally illegal, license plates from another vehicle, and no insurance. We headed out west again. We settled in Edmonton. At Christmas time I visited my brother Ted in Edmonton. I got drinking; my brother Ted kept feeding me whiskey with the intentions of getting me drunk. I did get drunk. I was not used to the frigid weather out there. I got very sick and was in bed for days, sweating and fighting to get well. I went into an altered state and I saw the twelve apostles looking down around me like an observation room, discussing whether I should continue to live or not!

As soon as I got somewhat well, we decided to head to a warmer climate. We sold everything we had and Ronnie, Marlene's brother, took the train up to join us from St. Catharines to make the trip back home. In my 1964 Chrysler still with the wrong plates and no insurance and a broken heater, we headed south intending to travel across the warmer parts of the States. We stopped at Canadian Tire and bought a propane tent burner to keep the car warm and together we drove across the border and the farther we drove south the better I felt. Out in the middle of the desert at night I began to see lights! I didn't know it at the time, but it was Los Vegas! As we got closer, the radio lit up with advertisements to come to their motel for a free bottle of Champaign. We stayed the night and I won six hundred dollars but stupid Ronnie and I blew it all in the next morning! As we traveled across the states the closer we got to home the colder it got. I still remember Ronnie and Darren fighting for the front seat for what little heat came out of the heater. We almost got home when our transmission went. We had to send for money from Marlene's parents. We got home the next evening and the next morning Marlene's brother, Gerald, had died on the couch, it was like he waited for us to come home. I was encouraged by my faith and so were they. Marcel used to say to me, you would make a good preacher. This was one of those events that I recognized a call of serving God revealing itself! I began to notice that people would gravitate to me for encouragement, answers, or advice. I'm not sure why but as time went on I would come to understand it was part of the purpose of my life.

It wasn't long after that we moved to Kitchener and lived on Greulke Street for a couple of years, the Chicopee Ski Hill was behind us. I remember this was a good time, Jim and Shelly and my sister Anne would come up to ski with us. We would go and visit my brother, Brent, in Brampton who was not too far from us. Tara was 4 and Darren was 15 years old. We got into skiing. Tara was always brave. I told her not to go on the ski lift and stay on the bunny hill but nothing frightened her. I turned around and there she was waving, "Hi Dad" on the Ski lift. Darren went to Eastwood High School, played football and made some friends there. Darren was at that rebellious age! He called me a name one day and he took off running, I couldn't catch him anymore. I waited until he came home and I jumped from the upstairs window on him and ripped his shirt by mistake. He was so disappointed about his shirt "Dad, you ripped my special shirt"! I really felt bad about that! I loved my kids and enjoyed being with them and we always had an atmosphere of joking and playing around. We got into mischief together as I was one of the kids growing up as well! Darren was not only my son but also my buddy. What ever we did, we usually did it together. In a way I was living out my youth, as I didn't have as a child. When I was into cars, scuba diving, music, guitars and dirt biking I got Darren and Tara into it as well. This was a pattern we kept through out our lives.

It wasn't long before we began to have financial problems again. I couldn't keep the hydro bill paid. So they cut my hydro off. When the neighbors would leave for work we would plug in to their outside hydro outlet and we could make tea and heat up food and water on a grill and wash and blow dry our hair. When it was starting to get cold in the house I decided to go out to the big green hydro box and connect the hydro myself. The hydro didn't like that much. They said I could have blown myself up. But I'll be damned if I was going to let my family go without. I wasn't going to lay down and let the world roll over me! We took a job as a family working at a group home called, Reality Homes for Children and became group home parents. I got back into playing guitar again. And I bought a new motorcycle. The relationship I had with my children began to change as my kids starting acting out, as they were one of the home's children. This wasn't what I felt my kids should be involved in so we resigned and got back together as a family and it wasn't long after that we joined the Salvation Army.

I thought of myself as a soldier going into a battle. My dad's family had been Salvation Army and I thought I would find a place working with the less fortunate. Marlene and I joined the Salvation Army. Both Marlene and I became soldiers in the Salvation Army. Tara began to play the recorder and together her and I sang and played the guitar. The poor captain didn't know what to do with me. He told me he was going to put reins on me and every time I would go ahead of him he would pull me back. He would get angry at me when I would ask him questions and bang the bible on the table and say if you are going to question one part, you have to question it all! The Salvation Army doesn't believe in water baptism and so I was baptized in a Missionary Church on November 16, 1980. I had been a Christian for three years. God was not without humor, at my baptism. I was very serious and when coming out of the baptism tank I expected to see doves, but what I saw was Darren lying on the floor killing himself laughing. Marlene was kicking him to be quiet. Apparently an old man had farted on the wooden bench and it echoed through the whole church.

I then attended Emmanuel Bible College. I loved the music and could sense the presence of the Holy Spirit in the songs. I found it difficult to survive without any money coming in. They had a food pantry at the college that kept us going. The students were a beautiful bunch of kids, word got around we couldn't pay our rent and they took up a collection for us. But in time my crude non-conformist, individualism personality spurred criticism in the older students I hung around with. They admitted to me one time that the Holy Spirit had convicted them for judging me. I found it more and more difficult to fit in! I began to look for a simpler way of life. I was seeking to be free of ties to earthly goods, or concern about them, dependence on them, and desire for them. I was beginning to question the fundamental religion, which seemed to be more interested in conforming me to their image and into the image of the middle-class and prosperity than they were in conforming me into the image of Christ! I saw Christ as a non-conformist. I was raised in a un-conformed counter cultural lifestyle. Trying now to fit in was not going to be easy. I began to attend a number of churches and charismatic groups, but I felt at odds. I tired quickly of preaching, after a while, words mingled into a silent drone of promises of prosperity for a donation.

The secular culture identity has to do with selfishness, money, power and materialism and to that end one throws all one's strength. The Spiritual is the opposite; it is simplicity, humbleness, and giving. What I saw when I went into the church was not distinctly separate! I saw a mixed value system. They were teaching the precepts of man as doctrine. I thought of myself as living in holy poverty; they just saw me as a bum. The Christians were against me! It was a culture shock for me. When I went to church I wasn't looking to be entertained. I wanted to worship God in holy silence. I felt that this middleclass religion had stolen Jesus from the poor! Anyone who wants to become part of this church would have to adapt to the middleclass society, not necessarily to Jesus! My experience with the church was they would rather I just went away. With or without the church and with or without their permission, I wasn't going away!

The Salvation Army Captain gave me a job bailing rags in the bottom of the thrift store. I couldn't stay in the basement tucked away, and would go upstairs to the hostel and talk to the men. Interestingly, there was a man working fixing items to be sold. He was a Jehovah witnesses, and we talked about God and his faith. Another well-meaning man from the Salvation Army gave me a job working in a bread factory. After a while I felt anxious and depressed. I felt God had brought me through all of this for a purpose. I felt called to work in God's service. Working for the man seemed meaningless without having a purpose to work for. I went up to the lunchroom on my break. And, sitting in front of me was a Bread of Life pamphlet. It was telling the story of Sir Francis Drake who after traveling the ocean seas ran into a storm as he was coming up the Thames River and almost sank. He stood on the bow of the boat and said: "I did not come this far to drown in this ditch!" I took that as a literal message for me. I saw myself as one like the fishermen when Jesus passed by the Sea of Galilee. Jesus said to them, "Come follow me, and I will make you fishers of men." Then they abandoned their nets and followed him. I in turn, abandoned what I was doing and walked out of the factory and went home. I realized I was called to preach the word, and not wait on tables. Marlene and I tried to push to find a place to serve God, even to the point of visiting the Salvation Army head office. After that I began to realize, I wasn't going to go any farther in the Army. After all, I went to the army to fight for the Lord; I wasn't there to conform to the world!

While I was attending Emmanuel Bible College, I had a few elderly ladies from the Jehovah Witnesses who would come and visit me at my home and we would talk about God and religion. I remember one of the kind old ladies said to the other one: "Larry talks to me more than my husband has talked to me in twenty years." Well, that night it was a cold night. I was to go to the house of the older students from the Bible College and study together. When I got there, the same old ladies were knocking on their door. "Hi, I said!" I was quite put out when the future pastors wouldn't let them in for even a minute to get warm because they were from a different faith. What would it have hurt to show a little kindness to a stranger? If anything, it would have proved right by showing love by their actions. After that I lost interest and couldn't continue to attend classes anymore. I never saw those future pastors again; I think they were just as happy to see me leave. Around the same time, I met a friend who was interested in talking about God. He invited me over to his home. When I got there his wife escorted me into the basement where the man was having a beer all by himself. Upstairs was the wife and his family. The man began to tell me how his father-in-law was a pastor, and how the whole family has rejected him and heaped all kinds of guilt and shame on him, because the man liked having a few beers. Here were well meaning people heaping guilt and fear in Jesus' name. I was bothered by this kind of legalism, or perfectionism. It takes love for a person to become anywhere near perfect. God is perfect in love! And, we are perfect when we act in love! Again, I think they would have been proved more right by their actions if they had shown love. We don't wait until we are perfect to love somebody; it is in loving others that makes us perfect. They should have loved him as he was, that is what Jesus would have done! Jesus had taken away my sins and guilt, and shame. Here was a guilt that was being imposed on the man and myself, a socially imposed guilt not a conviction of the Holy Spirit. All I knew was that, I was a sinner saved by grace! I live in a state of grace of God who saved me! Why do people work so hard and become so angry with people who don't conform to their ideals. In my way of thinking it was the individuals that change the world, never the conformist. I wouldn't consider Jesus to be a conformist. I had come to my own faith experience outside the church. I now felt like I was in a box, a box of conformity and someone else's identity. I didn't fit inside the box, and I began to look outside the box. I thought it was wrong that people conformed to the media ideals of the middleclass and media ideals of faith. I thought the middleclass was an evil concept to brain wash people to sell them their products and people were going in debt over their heads to keep up the image! Life was more than the amount of toys you have in the end!

In general, what disappointed me about religion was the superficiality of it. The church was interested in the ones who fit the bill, young, slim, educated, all of the requirements of a worldly corporation. I became discouraged and began to dislike Christians. I was on a different journey and I decided to separate myself from them. I was tired of the hell and brimstone preaching with the sole purpose of convicting the person and breaking the person down into submission. That is all right for some, perhaps even needed. But, I had already been through my own conversion. I felt I just couldn't live up to their expectations. I was seeking a way of serving God in love. I learned valuable imperial experiences that taught me never to be critical, and always be loving, positive and encouraging. But, having said that, I think it is part of the journey! We mask ourselves in acts of self-righteousness and piety to cover our own insecurities and fears.

But again, I was encouraged. I fell asleep in the afternoon. I had a vision; it was Peter Salzmann's picture of Jesus. Jesus turned his eyes and stared straight at me, wow! I jumped up and I went for a walk across a field. I came to a United Church and I walked in. I met the Pastor Melvin Rose and we talked about Jesus, and religion. As Melvin and I talked, I saw a different view of what I had seen in the fundamental, literal, conservative translation of the bible. Melvin opened my eyes to the symbolic interpretation of scripture and the literal translation took on new meaning. I looked above his head and there was the picture I had seen in my vision.

We became friends with Melvin and his wife Julia. One thing he pointed out to me was that in Genesis when God finished creating the world he said: "It was good!" Man is basically good! I began to see that the Christian life should be one that people look for the good in each other! Then we will see God in each other! The Christian life should be filled with love, hope and positive thinking. I saw no point in looking for the negative in each other! I could no longer call myself a fundamentalist!

I joined the United Church of Canada and applied to Waterloo University as a mature student, and began the process of ordination. We moved to Waterloo and rented a condominium. One particular event I remember very clearly was when I was at home alone and I was praying in the bedroom. I smelled the most beautiful scent. My immediate sense was this is the presence of Jesus and the oil the women poured on Jesus' feet! We got a job as superintendent running a condominium at the same time that I went to Waterloo University. I was particularly interested and took extended courses in dream psychology. It was a good time. I enjoyed studying and learning, and in my spare time I would play Christian songs on my guitar in preparation for ministry.

Marlene was becoming increasingly unhappy in the marriage and decided she didn't want any more children and had an operation not to have any more. She woke one night to tell me she kept having a recurring dream that she was pregnant. One day about eight months later, Marlene, got a call from the doctor to tell her she was pregnant. She couldn't believe it and said: "No, you are mistaken. I had my tubes tied, cut and burned eight months ago!" Sure enough, she was pregnant.

It was at that time we received my first call to a two-point parish, in a small town called Holstein. We moved into the manse of the Holstein United Church on July 1st, 1983. We moved in that afternoon, and I was informed that an elderly lady had died and I was expected to perform my first funeral! Marlene went into labor and I rushed her into the hospital in Mount Forest. Nathan was born in the early morning of July 2, 1983. Marlene was 36 years old. I was tired from preparing for the funeral and taking Marlene to the hospital and performing my first burial and sermon that I was just too tired to be present when Marlene gave birth. Marlene never forgave me for putting the church people first. Unfortunately, I didn't do well as being the minister! Don't get me wrong; I was grateful for the experience. We stayed for a year there and left. Marlene didn't want to be involved with the church people and resented them! Marlene always said: "She didn't marry a minister!" Darren did not want to go to church, and he chained himself to a desk. So I carried him and the desk to church. This was a great way to get your kids to church to teach them about the love of God! We laugh at it now. Darren did tell me however about a time when he was in the church, he felt God pass through him. I was disappointed that I could not have done better. It was a tough year for all of us! I was frustrated. I heard God say: "Be still and know that I am God!" I have nothing against the good people of Holstein. I just didn't fit in there. After that year, we all moved back to Kitchener. I received a letter from the United Church telling me that square pegs are all right and round pegs are alright but round pegs don't fit into square holes and they withdrew me from the roles.

We then moved back to St. Catharines. I began to attend the Concordia Lutheran Seminary for a short time. I came home in the afternoon and fell asleep. I awoke to a vision. I saw in front of me a stone hut, it had a wooden door. I opened the door and there sitting in the middle of the floor was Jesus. His hair was long and straight and greasy. (This wasn't the middle-class Jesus usually seen on the walls of the church. Later, I took that to mean I was called to the poor!) I went over and laid my head on his lap. He took dirt from the ground floor and put it on the side of my head. He said to me: "Larry, your problem is perfectionism!" I was beginning to experience problems of compulsive behavior. This kind of behavior comes when there is something in our head that tells us it isn't good enough, and one gets the compulsion to do it over and over again. I fought my compulsive behaviors. This was one of my first lessons in humbleness; I began to accept that which was less than perfect. In humbleness, I took on a penitent heart. I stopped worrying about being perfect and accepted the weaknesses within me. I began a life of simplicity. I began wanting to have less than the best. I began to live in the moment, in the presence of God. I learned to have a short-term plan for the future but not live in the future. I learned to live in hope, in the present, in the grace of God, which is sufficient for the day. The devil has preoccupied the world with materialism and worry. The heart must be free of ties to earthly goods, of concern about them, dependence on them, desire for them, if it is to belong and serve the divine. I learned to be grateful for each day, and live each moment. What a difference it made in my life to wake up each morning and thank and praise the Lord, and ask him to come and be in me, through me, and around me. And, live in hope and optimism each moment of the day. Apostle Paul said: "I know I am wasting away on the outside but I know each day we are being renewed on the inside!"

Perfection can be a disease that cripples a person deeply as any ailment! When perfectionism got a hold on me, I started thinking I had to become perfect before I could do anything and in the end, end up doing nothing. I stopped playing my guitar for I thought I wasn't good enough. I became a loner because I didn't feel others would accept me! When Jesus said: "Be perfect as your heavenly Father is perfect." I am sure he meant to be perfect in love. God works in our weakness. God didn't take my weaknesses from me he taught me to accept them and learn to live with them. There is great strength in our weaknesses. God didn't take Paul's thorn in the flesh away from him; he used it to keep Paul humble and to be aware of his sin, and need of forgiveness and dependence on our Lord. His grace is sufficient for us! I realized in my life that I am at my worst, when I get caught up in trying to be perfect. When I look back, I am ashamed of the times I have made anyone feel less of a person by my own self-righteousness and attempts at perfectionism! I attended the Seminary for a term and didn't do well; I applied to become an army chaplain but was refused.

We moved back to Kitchener. Darren moved out on his own when he met Michele. Darren met Michele in a Pentecostal Church in Kitchener. He was turned off the church and never went back again when they told him he was spiritually dead. Drawn by the liturgy and the communion I began to attend an Anglican church. I was becoming more depressed and discouraged. I was still dealing with constant fear within me. I felt so much anxiety and fear I went into the bathroom to be alone, I kept the bible in there. I just opened the bible anywhere and fixed my eyes on a particular passage to my amazement. It was Jesus speaking: He said: "Do not fear; just believe!" Jesus taught me to live one day at a time. Even more than one day at a time one moment at a time, in the presence and grace of the Holy Spirit. I asked God to take the fear from me, but it remained! I believe God allowed this to continue to be part of my life for a reason not yet understood at that time!

I began thinking perhaps I could serve God apart from the church. Perhaps, in journalism I could do some good. I decided to go to Conestoga College to study Journalism. But again something would happen to encourage me to continue in ministry. My first assignment in the journalism class was to interview a man who had lost it all and was living in his car. To make a long story short. I couldn't see the sense in just writing about something. It was just words without action. I again felt I needed to be in the position to help and encourage in the love of God. I didn't continue in College. I decided to try the church again! I went to a retreat in Toronto, to attend an information session on the Anglican Church Army in an attempt to fit in but people size you up quickly! People are quick to reject you; if not immediately, if you don't fit their ideals. To the Anglicans etiquette seemed to be the most important thing. I had a lady come to me and tell me she didn't like the way I dressed. She said I should wear underwear. I was embarrassed and left the retreat! I curse the day I tried to belong. I am done with trying to belong. I wasn't going to fit into the ministry, at least not in the established church! I had attempted and failed. I struggled with myself. I am crude at times. I don't mean to be, I was raised alone to defend for myself and I had been raised in reform schools, holding centers, on the streets and on welfare, where would I have learned etiquette?

I had to go into Conestoga College to sign a paper to have my student loan transferred. The lady who looks after it called me into her office to review my student loan. She was a comically grumpy older lady. I noticed a few clippings on her cubicle that were religious in orientation but I didn't get into anything about her religion but we seem to talk to one another as if we had known each other before. There was a oneness and a warmness right from the beginning. She seemed interested in my life. I told her that I really wanted to be a minister, and that I had been a minister for a whole year but realized that I could not fit in. She began to open up to me about her journey and she told me how she also couldn't fit in. She began to tell me that although she wasn't a religious person she also considered herself a spiritual person and went on to tell me how she belonged to a spiritual group that associates with Edgar Casey the Prophet. I knew of Edgar Casey from my earlier years of searching; I had read his biography. We talked of dreams, religion, doing good and love. The conversation was not all that interesting but I felt good inside, warm, there was a connection, and I know she felt the same. I know I brightened her day and she brightened mine, but just how that was done, or why it was done, only God knows. Perhaps it was done for just the reason to show there is loving, spiritual, people outside the church. God is with us all. I was encouraged to think that I could perhaps find a way of belonging maybe through a spiritual magazine for an example! I guess the point was that I was opening my mind to the possibilities of expressing my faith in ways unknown to me at the time.

CHAPTER FOUR

"Separation and Divorce"

MARLENE AND I were increasingly at odds with each other and it became more and more difficult to keep it together. After I became a Christian, I had confessed of my previous unfaithfulness of my teenager years. Marlene never forgave me and held it in her heart to get even. She started to take trips to her sisters in Thorold. And, one day confessed she took revenge on me and was intimate with a person I knew. The pain devastated me. But, it was my own fault.

I was so lost and not sure what to do. I didn't know if I wanted to fight for the marriage or let it go! I had spent many nights on the couch; sleepless, wishing this situation could come to an end. I had no hope of any success, unless I had someone who worked along side of me. Marlene had no intentions to do that! Marlene wanted to date other men. She wanted to live what she thought she missed in her youth. I was depressed; it was not that I was mad at Marlene, I was just depressed at the hopelessness of the situation. If there was hope that she would change it could be different but as it is Marlene refuses even to look at the situation without getting angry, reversing the situation or changing the subject, or look the other way, or blame me for each and every situation. She refuses to take any responsibility for her own life. She has a lot of difficulty in looking after Nathan and finds it hard to discipline him. When I discipline Nathan then she takes his side. Life has become very difficult. She is forever reminding me of the things I have done wrong in my life. I'm always being accused of flirting, which is untrue. Marlene finds everything to be a hassle even everyday events to her are a problem, even things like people visiting us, visiting my own family, even going for supper usually turns into a frustration. Nathan is discouraged about having friends in. In general she is moody, explosive, critical, uncooperative, frustrated. It was very apparent that what Marlene is doing is starting these fights to create a scene, she will bring something up that happened ten years ago, or she will create an imaginary situation out of nothing and put emotions to it to create a situation of tension in which I must defend myself. She fights me all the way. She will fight me in every thing I do. Whenever I talk, I am talked over, or she will challenge me. She likes to get Darren or others to prove me wrong. It is obvious that she is unhappy and regrets living my life as she puts it. She is reluctant to help me and is not interested in a future. In frustration I eat and drink more than the normal, and I have put on a lot of weight. I was not the handsome man I was when I first met her! Marlene wanted to date other men. She wanted to live what she thought she missed in her youth. I felt I had no control over my life and I was growing more and more frustrated and angry!

One time in a parking lot I wasn't going fast enough for some guy and he yelled at me and called me a nasty name! I came up behind him and his girlfriend in their new BMW convertible and, with my van, I pushed his car into the intercession. The guy wasn't so mouthy after that. We took off home before the cops came and laughed our heads off all the way home! Another time I was just driving down the road when a guy came flying up beside me and called me a fag! That anger within me was aroused again. I chased him into a gas station, and as I got out he pulled a gun out of his belt. I punched him and knocked him down and jumped in my car and took off. Later I called the police. The police told me that he had just robbed a service station and was pulling in that station to rob another. But, the cop told me that since you hit him he took off home and after a stand off he was arrested! The point of me telling these incidences is that I was starting to act out in my anger!

Our personalities worked against each other and nothing was achieved. I was convinced I was doomed if I didn't get out of this relationship with Marlene. We both agreed we didn't have anything in common. We got into another fight and she agreed to leave. After not talking to me for three days. She broke her silence and asked me if I wanted a cup of tea. I told her we could always be friends but she would still have to leave. She asked me if I really wanted her to move. I told her that since we don't get along it would be the best idea. She went into the bedroom. I felt sorry for her. But, anybody in his or her right mind would have ended it a long time ago. If it only happened once in a while it would be normal, but it happened so often that many precious days were wasted in nonsense. And if anything, made me feel guilty. When it came for her to leave Marlene had the car packed and ready to go. Both of us kept stalling and we made up. But it wasn't too long before Marlene and I ran up against the same brick wall. I had to accept that Marlene loved me as a friend but she was not in love with me, yet I have been in love with her. She couldn't give anymore than a friend had to give. She couldn't give me the love, intimacy, bonding, and commitment that I needed. I had a dream: Marlene was on a sailboat, sailing it herself. In other words: She is sailing on her own! I remember waking that morning thinking: "I wish the separation didn't happen but it did!"

Eventually, Marlene and Tara moved to St. Catharines and began their own lives. I stayed in Kitchener and Nathan stayed with me. The hope of living by myself meant to me I might gain control over my own destiny. For the first time in a long I began to settle in one place and I began to accept the fact I was a single father! I applied for Father's allowance and became Mr. Mom. I cooked the meals, got Nathan to school, and cleaned the apartment. Marlene and I always remained in touch. In the love of the Lord we were able to forgive each other. We divorced after 22 ½ years of marriage. I was 41 years old. Yet, after the divorce Marlene and I were still seeing each other and being intimate. Marlene would come up to Kitchener and see Nathan; and I would often go to see Marlene in St. Catharines. My heart would break each time I saw her and I knew she was with others. When we got together usually to see the children, we would have a romantic time together. She told me once, the reason you are intimate with me is because you don't feel guilty with me! It was true! True love casts out fear! Yet, I knew it was over and I knew we had to move on with our lives. The last time we got together we talked the whole day like we talked so many times before. We concluded that we really didn't have what could be called a marriage, in fact we were divorced. Marlene and I had what is best described as a convenient and romantic relationship. We helped each other financially. Nathan is being raised with both a mother and father, and we had companionship and romance. But, it ends there. There was no commitment. Marlene really was not the marrying kind. She does not want the relationship to resemble a marriage. Marlene and I do not share anything; we are complete opposites and are destructive for each other. We relate to each other by drinking with each other. But, even when we drank we argued. Opposites attract, perhaps this is why we are attracted to each other but there is no way we should have been married in the first place. She told me she thought I would find someone else someday. The annulment finally ended all intimacy!

The hurt of the divorce stayed with me for a long time and even to this day a common thread that flows through my dreams is one of abandonment. It seems I was destined to be left alone from the beginning of my life. My divorce from Marlene was something that influenced me for my whole of life. In my dreams, I was regretfully leaving a woman and her child. To feel a great sadness within me that I go looking for her never to find her . . . I'm in a four-wheel truck trying to jump or climb a big hill only to fall back again . . . *my life*! I find myself in a Catholic Church rectory . . . two teens are there . . . I have the feeling I am just passing through . . . *insecurity*! I have my guitar and the teens ask me to sing Alleluia; which we sing together . . . in their car I meet a pastor and his wife or a priest and women they are asking me for directions to Midland . . . I give directions . . . . *my purpose*! I have my motorcycle, I'm feeling lost and alone and not sure what route to take to find the woman and her child. I met a man who agrees to give me directions! (*Jesus*)

But we were still a family; we still had children to raise! Over the years and through it all, we came to be trusted friends. Someone I truly trust! People couldn't understand why I would be a friend with my ex-wife, but they were the only true and trusted friends and family I knew! To this day Marlene's family still treat me like a family member and call me uncle Larry. Marlene met Rob from Nova Scotia. Rob and Willie were friends and they dated Marlene and Tara. After all these years we have all become good friends, more than friends, we are all tried and trusted members of a family. I give thanks for them and pray for them everyday. If it weren't for Rob and Marlene, Darren and Tara; Nathan and I would have starved. Marlene always kept in touch and made sure Nathan had what he needed.

CHAPTER FIVE

"The Lord is my Shepherd"

ON NOVEMBER 26, 1990 I started a journal. I felt I needed to be alone and to think, to understand my own feelings, desires, purpose and my own restlessness. My journal became my companion. I literally poured out my heart out on my computer and through the years I sorted my life out! I had a great sense of adventure in my youth; I loved to travel and rarely stayed in one place. I struggled with restlessness and conformity for years. When I was in Hamilton I met a minister who shed light on my restlessness. He said he could see that I was nomadic. He went on to explain that in my historical genetics I belong to a nomadic clan, people who traveled with the herds. He went on to say that the nomads were quite different than the townsfolk. The nomads took nothing with them and traveled light, lived simply and didn't settle down.

I realized that whenever I traveled I didn't escape anything for I took myself with me! I had been a rolling stone most of my life simply because I have not found anywhere to belong. As time progressed I found no adventure just roaming around the country without any purpose to it all. But in comparison when I see what the average man has to give of himself to be a conformist; I consider myself a lucky man. You would think that I would have found a place of belonging along the way. It is not that I have not tried; I have made many attempts. From the beginning of my religious journey, before my religious journey, from the beginning of my life I have always been out of sync, a fish out of water, a weed amongst the roses. There was a weed growing in my flowerbed on my balcony, it reminded me of me. No one knows where it came from, it just appeared, and it looked out of place. I had some guests the other day and they wanted to pluck the weed out! "No!" I said. "Let it grow and it became tall." I thought this represented myself. Standing alone let us see what I become! I preferred to be like the weed and grow on my own.

I observed three teen girls walking together; two of the girls were close together laughing with each other but the one girl was by herself looking onto the other girls. I could tell she wanted to be accepted by the other two, and I felt sorry for the lone girl. I thought if a person could get over the desire to be accepted one may be happier as an individual rather than conforming!

On the inside I felt like I was working toward Sainthood but on the outside I looked unacceptable, at least in society's eyes. It is obvious that trying to change my life is next to impossible and acceptance is now the way to go. I believe it's time to accept my own destiny. I thought the best thing for me is to forget about conformity and try to find ways of serving God outside the church, find a way of making a living that gives me a sense of purpose. I consider myself blessed by God and a lucky man to have what I have! I feel that it is obvious that I will never fit in the church society, and the community. I feel I would be much better off to carve out my own path and identity. It is obvious that my family including myself learn best when we approach things with hands on approach, empirical experience rather than traditional teachings. I live by one simple philosophy; Christ enters into our hearts; and out of the heart comes the good God has planted. We become God's hands and feet, eyes and compassion.

I thought it important to discover Jesus on my own! What I saw was a homeless Jesus who left the ninety nine and came looking for the one who was lost, who had nowhere to lay his head, a poor Jesus who:

- Carried only what he needed, who desired not possessions,
- Claimed the poor were blessed!
- Said it was hard for a rich man to get into the Kingdom,
- Turned over tradition!
- Was a radical!
- Told his disciples to go into the world and preach the Gospel and take nothing with them!

This is quite different than the preachers of today who are preaching a prosperity Gospel! The poor Jesus isn't a very popular view of Christ. But, I felt that this is what I was called to, to give all, to be a disciple! As I saw it, the less I had, the happier I became and the holier I felt. The more I rejected this world, the closer I became to Jesus. I had found my purpose! I found it more and more difficult to relate to the established religion of the day. I began to feel that religion had gone astray! The first Christians met and broke bread in their homes. Acts: 4:32-35, 2:42. And they had everything in common and helped each other as they had need. I felt I needed to go back to the life of the early Christians. There is a big difference between those early Christians and the church of today. I was awakened to the truth and the truth set me free. If and when you come to Christ be careful of religion! There are many who will take advantage of religion and you for their own gain. They will tell you want you want to hear and promise you wealth and prosperity. God comes in humbleness as a child. You will recognize God in the simple, and the humble.

I dropped Nathan off at the Bedard family for Christmas. Rachael asked us down for a Christmas meal, and after it was over we all left and I could tell that she was feeling alone and sad and almost cried when we left. I kissed her when I left, I wish I could have asked her to come with us but I knew it would have started a fight with Marlene. We then went to Clem and Debbie's home. Nathan called me while I was there and told me that the conclusion of "The story of the Christ Child", that we had been watching, was on TV. There was a silence for a while, and I asked if they had watched it, I already knew that they hadn't for they had made fun of religion in the past, and I knew I was wasting my time trying to say anything about God. Clem responded sarcastically, saying he doesn't watch too much religious programs, and Debbie responded by saying she had to read the God damn bible to the old people where she works as a nurse's aide.

We then went to my brother Steven and Patsy's house for the Goodnough family Christmas dinner. My father was invited but was reluctant in coming over for he was disappointed that he couldn't get his girlfriend Norren to come. There wasn't any talk of the Christ child or prayer before dinner. Brent brought his daughter from his old girl friend named Faye. When we were by ourselves I talked quite a bit with her, she told me she was afraid that she was going to die. I asked her why would God bring her into this world only to let her die? We became friends and she hugged me before I left, and told me she felt more like a Goodnough then the family she had been raised with! I felt for her.

We returned home on the evening of the twenty-sixth and that night I had a dream: I was sitting around a table with a guy, individual type person. Darren was there. This guy was talking of a German word to describe emptiness in ones heart not described in English. I said to this fellow that the Evangelist Billy Graham had described this feeling as a vacuum in ones heart. I then began to tell with great difficulty how I had this feeling in my heart at one time but had gone through an experience with God that had filled the vacuum. I felt guilty in my dream. I was convinced in the dream that I had a calling! In some way I was feeling guilty or embarrassed by the events that happened with my family dinners. I felt that I should have said something about God to help my family find themselves; they all seem lost to me. It takes one to know one! I realized these feelings or calling were imbedded in me and was not going to go away. I am going to feel this way all my life, until I do something!

Unfortunately, for the next couple of years it was a sad time in our family for there were a few deaths. I continued to write in my journal and looked after Nathan. I attended an Anglican church while in Kitchener. For a short time I began to attend a fundamental church called Harvest

Ministries. Marlene's sister Debbie's husband Clem was dying. She asked me if I would come and pray for Clem. He had fought a long battle with cancer. Debbie and Clem were good to us when we used to travel. Once when we came back from a trip to Florida on a bus, they were the first to pick us up and take us in. Clem wasn't a religious person but I think he was encouraged with me because through it all I kept my faith. I drove down from Kitchener with a friend who attended the same church. When I got to the hospital Clem had already died and this fanatical person with me wanted to pray for Clem to raise him from the dead! He angered me with his blind faith; how cruel it would have been after all the suffering they had already gone through.

I attended a singles group at the same church and when I sat down in the group a lady started praying that there was an evil spirit among them there. It was obvious they were talking about me and I just left. I had a pastor come over for some encouragement. But, all I got was criticism! The fanatical Christians who live by blind faith disturbed me. It scares me to think how false prophets of a prosperity gospel could mislead them. When I see the television evangelist it is like a nightmare, when I think that this the first impression of God the people outside of the church see. God has been manipulated for power and profit and control from the beginning of the faith!

Marlene's family talked with me about God before they died, Amanda and Marcel, Amy and Gloria who always talked about God and Forest Lawn. All have past on now. I remember also Marlene's grandmother that we used to go and visit her in the Bestview Home for the ageing. One particular time I had put on a white sweater and then at the last minute I changed it and wore a red one. When we got there she said she had a dream about us last night and I knew you would come and visit me today and Lorry, as she called me, was wearing a red sweater!

I reluctantly included this paragraph as an example of how important it is that we forgive each other; and above all don't hold anything negative in our hearts. Amanda and Marcel were good to me. But I was taken back by her negativity in life and tried to understand why. I found out that one of her children had died at the hands of a drunk driver. She couldn't forgive or forget and she held anger in her heart. In their love for their children they became over protected and critical. Marlene's personality is a result of that overprotection and negativity. Negative thinking brings all kinds of evil into our lives, sickness, fear, hatred, and it robs those around us who need our love. After Amanda, Marlene's mom, died Darren had an interesting dream, a huge angry man took Darren under ground (hell) into a room and lying on a stone slate table was Amanda. The man lifted his hand and Darren said the man's hand was huge as he pointed his finger at Amanda. He was angry, despised and pissed at grandma. And said: "Don't let that negativity enter into your children!"

We moved back to St. Catharines again. Nathan and I were just living on Father's Allowance at the time. I was accepted at McMaster Divinity College. I would drive up to Hamilton for classes. But, I was unable to keep up my studies; I just couldn't afford to go! I had a hunger for God. I had a strong desire to serve the Lord. But, how would I ever do it? I was drinking more and more and often went to class with a hangover. It was lonely times and I was walking around in a fog. If anyone has gone through a death or divorce you could relate. I attended St. Alban's Anglican Church. I don't remember how but I joined a music ministry.

It was healing to sing; and members of the music group sensed my pain of divorce and were good to me. The Priest Rev. Patty Dorian called me the "Gatekeeper". I still don't know why! Before I stopped studying, I told one of the parishioners I was studying at McMaster and he told me it would not be for another 10 years before I would make it to ministry. He was wrong, it was going to take me a lot longer than that.

Most of my struggle back in the day was just to survive. I spent most of my time looking after Nathan, and grateful when we had a place to live. When Nathan went to school and I was alone my thoughts turned inward towards the depth of my own loneliness. I had been a married man for twenty-two years and had been intimate and then nothing. Although still young, at least in heart. My thoughts were clouded in passion. I wasn't the handsome man I used to be and I couldn't get by on my looks anymore. I had put a lot of weight on. No doubt trying to fill the loneliness of my heart with food and drink. I thought if I could only find someone to love me everything would be fine with the world. My hope was to find someone who related to me and loved and wanted to serve God. But like Job you don't have many friends when you are a man without means. I attended a singles group in St. Catharines for a while and then another time I went to a Christian Singles group. One of the men came up to me to tell me; I was there just to fornicate and get the women pregnant! I left! I dated others for a while and I met some nice women but was uncomfortable and felt I was doing something wrong! I was so nervous around women. I remember a time when I took a lady to dinner at Red Lobster. I was so nervous that my nose began to bleed. The only love I found was of the conditional kind. I would call it commercial love! Bought and sold to the highest bidder! In time, I felt holier if I stayed away from women. It didn't happen all at once but circumstances led me to be more interested in the mind set of celibacy and turned down opportunities to be intimate with woman. But the thought that someday I might meet that someone special stayed in my mind and heart. My thoughts turned more towards the love of God and His world and His creatures. I'm not sure why or how but my heart's desire had changed, I no longer seeked to be loved but to love! With the eyes of the love of God I could see that much of our world suffers from the lack of the true unconditional love of God. Especially the ones others reject, the wounded, the lonely, the ugly, the poor and the lowly.

We moved to Niagara Falls, I'm not sure why but I think because Marlene moved there and Nathan needed to be near his mom. I began to attend St. Stephens Anglican Church. Bishop Clarence confirmed me into the Anglican Church. The church is now closed down. And in a way that is what happened to me. I was a broken soul and I just closed down also! I couldn't bring myself to go to any church anymore. What was the point; I wasn't going to find a way through the churches? But I never gave up on my belief that God had called me to do ministry.

Larry's famous rock, I use to sit on all the time and the railway crossing in the background

Sister Lana, Cousin Jimmy, Cousin Eleanor on a visit from Midland.

Larry and Mom in Oshawa   Our House, Mom, Lana, and Ted.

Larry and Marlene Married At Age 18   Larry and Marlene and Darren

Larry Mom and Brent's first re-union

Larry's Ordination: Archbishop Mullan, Fr. Luke, and Fr. Del

Fr. Larry, Bryan and Alissa's Wedding Ceremony

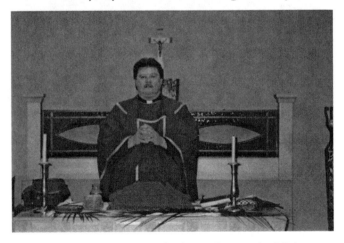

Rev. Fr. Larry – Franciscan Lutheran Community Ministry

CHAPTER SIX

"The Good Samaritan Mission"

ONE DAY AS I was driving I noticed a closed down Taco Bell Restaurant. I saw a Taco Bell Mission! From that time on the idea of a mission was planted in my heart! I also attended the Salvation Army in Niagara Falls for a while when I was also attending St. Stephen's Anglican. I met a good friend Larry Holden. We often talked about God and attended some home bible studies. We reflected that Jesus was a poor man with poor man's values, helping each other, serving each other. I believe what happens is that when people become wealthier they become more selfish and the church begins to compromise and so the middleclass church has become confused between basic values, or the true teachings of Jesus and middle class values or social standards. I believe the poor are refusing to go to church because they feel judged and made to conform to the image of the church or society rather than to the image of God. I believe people are looking to go back to the basics of the poor Jesus and his values. The early church began by people meeting in each other's houses. I thought to myself perhaps this idea could be the beginning of a new church! I can see myself either working in a missionary position within the Salvation Army or beginning a church away from all previous traditions! It very well may be the only way to get back to the basics.

I went to the Salvation Army Bible Study picnic one evening and got into a conversation with a retired Salvation Army officer, Major Woods. We talked about my call to missions and he confirmed in me what I believed was true. He told me to simply go and open a down town mission! He told me that I wouldn't find much help through any organization! He in fact told me that if I were to become an Auxiliary Captain, for I was considering it, I would be under their rules and would find that the bureaucracy would indeed hinder me rather than help me. He said he would help me and ask in prayer for a way to get financing. I couldn't get to sleep that night for I was thinking of how I could get a mission started on my own! I believe in faith that if I got a mission started I would find support! I believe I can sell the mission to the local churches and possibly get some support that way. Restaurants and grocery stores could give day old food etc. I thought we could fix things and resell them to help support the mission. My mind was swimming with all the possibilities!

I invited some Christians to come over to my apartment and I officially announced that I was starting a missionary drive. I had twenty something people from different denominations and I burned myself out from talking. Reception went well with most but some thought that I should stay where I am and do the same thing through the Army Others where concerned that I didn't have a denominational cover or a doctrinal statement but most were for it as long as Christ was at the head of it all. One of the ladies invited us to use her home for our next meeting in a week's time. I realized the need to address all denominations; I needed to find a way of expressing both the protestant and catholic faith, which has been possible within the Anglican tradition community. I was invited to two different lady's homes for lunch and supper. One was a fundamentalist and I was constantly defending myself as she is the more aggressive one, and the other a catholic I feel at home with her, knowing that her view of God is a loving God not a condemning God. They have trouble with my liberal way of thinking and make the assumption that I'm somehow going to fall or are teaching false or new wave religion. I didn't receive any real help and I grew tired of words and trying to convince people to help with a mission and decide to do it on my own!

With my son Darren's help we opened the store on Main Street in Niagara Falls. I have decided to call the mission "The Good Samaritan Mission" for it is the sinner, the outcast, the Samaritan that demonstrates true love by helping his neighbor. Two of the girls from the Bertie Brethren in Christ Church came to help. Mike and Donnie both Samaritans are helping me tomorrow to tear down walls and paint while the religious walk on by. I hadn't heard anything from my friend, Larry; he had gotten married lately, and so I didn't blame him. I was quite shocked when I heard that Larry had a heart attack and died! I attended his funeral at the Salvation Army.

We placed ads in the newspaper, collected used clothes, and toys, anything people would give. We helped a lot of people. There were lots of stories. The newspaper wrote an article about us. I met Deacon Shawn when my daughter got married at St. Georges Anglican Church. The good Bishop Goodrich offered to let us use the basement and kitchen of St. George's. We had dinners for the needy, prepared by the needy; we had toy drives for the children at Christmas. One person donated a new Nintendo game machine. My daughter, Tara, begged me to give it to her for her children but I lingered! As I gave out the gifts I asked each child what they were getting for Christmas? One of the boys was not getting anything and so I said to the boy; I will give you this larger gift for your smaller gift and of course he said yes. Tara was a little put out! After the children had left, we heard a loud thumping coming down the stairs, a robust lady came running across the hall and hugged Tara and said: "Thank you, Thank you, we had nothing for Christmas for him"! Tara looked at me with tears in her eyes. One look said it all!

But the most interesting story was when my brother, Stephan, got some information about our brother, Richard. We had been searching for him for forty years. Stephen was very instrumental in trying to find Richard and Lana. We made trips to Toronto whenever we got a new lead. We went to the Library in Toronto searching for a car dealership that Richard's adopted Father supposedly had owned! Stephen got the idea of sending away a letter to the government birth department, and they sent back a letter asking for a signature of the father. Dad signed and sent it back. A letter came addressed to Richard LePan. It sat on my dad's tables for weeks and then one day Stephen noticed it and opened it. And quickly figured out this was our brother by the same birth date. We looked up a Lepan in Toronto and got a hold of some friends who were living with Richard. I said to my brothers should we write a letter before we go? My brothers would have nothing to do with sending a letter and went to visit him that night. Brent and Stephen agreed; let's just go! It was Richard's birthday on April 14th. Interestingly, the year before I had taken note in my journal if we don't find him by April 14th I wasn't going to look for him anymore.

We assumed Richard was wealthy so we dressed up a little and went to visit him in suits! Later he told me that when he saw us on the apartment video camera he thought us three big guys were from the mafia. We knocked at his door armed with all our proof of him being our brother. We asked are you Richard LePan he reluctantly said "yes," "Well, we believe you are our brother!" After we presented our proof it was our brother! Richard never knew he had brothers and sisters. Well, off come the suits and we went out with Richard to the bar and met all of his friends. Later, Richard moved to St. Catharines and we have been close ever since.

Richard became friends with Marlene's sister. Rachelle came close to death and wrote me a letter of her experience with Jesus and the angel before she died of cancer. I was privileged to lead Rachael to the Lord when in the middle of the night she would call me and talk. What follows is her letter she wrote to me:

"As I lay in that hospital bed, I was bleeding badly, I knew I was dying and I was afraid. I looked at the time and it was 3:30 a.m. Then, in front of me was a light, like a white sun. I could feel the warmth. Then, I was sucked out of my body and I was very, very much afraid. No, I can't leave. I have to fight to go back I thought. The guardian angel kept me alive but told me I had to die. The light was much brighter than light to me, and the beam was love.

Then the light reached out and embraced me. It was Jesus Christ the Lord. He had one sense of humor. He said everything would be okay Rachelle. Hold on, believe me or not! I was taken to the most beautiful garden I had ever seen. Water drops where falling down from the mountains and the living water would always pray. God showed me the most beautiful flowers that opened up to me with love. The dear Lord showed me that I had to grow up in love like those flowers. I had to come to that level. I never, ever thought that the beautiful Lord Jesus Christ would ever want me to go this way.

Rachelle you have the desire only God would know. The pain was so great sometimes I thought I was in hell! I have always felt that life wasn't fair because I was so small and under so much weight. There were many, many times I had tried to kill myself but I had seen the demons. It was about much love in each one of us. It was God's love living within us. I told him I wanted to please come back. Then the person who came down to me had a beautiful white gown. I knew it was the angel because she came into my body and let me go. I am not very strong but I will do it for my love ones. My dad always said be strong you will make it, love on your own. I will fight it all the way, I lost my dad and my brother Benny to cancer and recently I lost my brother in law and my mother.

Then I got to the point that I was a freak but I am very close to God because He is the only one keeping me alive.

I will always remember it so well and I was very, very upset much more then you would ever know. It took me a long time to tell my family because they would for sure think I was crazy. I love my whole family and much, much more and I would never hurt any of them. One thing I could never, never do is to erase history because I am everybody that loves me. I would give my family and everyone my love plus to you precious Mandy. I like to reach out and help people in need because life is love. My prayers go up to heaven. I have to reach out to the light. It will always be me and myself."

But, now the devil has his turn, for every action there is an equal and opposite reaction! The landlord from Toronto phoned me and started to lay into me about people in the building and others where complaining they were worried about me bringing rift raft in the neighborhood. The neighborhood is a red light district! I hit the wall again. The social services found out I had a business and they cut me off. My rent went into arrears, my telephone was about to be cut off. I hadn't any more money to continue in the store! I had no choice but to close down.

Without finances, it wasn't long before I lost my apartment and we became homeless. Nathan, I and our dog Joey, ended up living in my van, in Marlene's driveway What was sad for Nathan is that Marlene let us come into her apartment only if he gave his dog away. Since we didn't have a residence we were ineligible for welfare. The next struggle was now with Social Services! Eventually, we did get back on Fathers' Allowance and Nathan and I moved into an apartment in Thorold. So much for trying to do good! We went looking for his dog, Joey, but were unable to find him. I was discouraged, how would we ever survive, let alone fulfill my desire to serve the Lord!

At that time it seemed to me the whole world does nothing but hurt and repress you. I felt like Captain Nemo again and I began to withdraw from the world. I just wanted to live by myself, seeking the good things in God. Each time I reached out in my loneliness the world turned ugly, depressing, hurtful and cruel and I withdrew into myself.

In the words of Dante "In the middle of my life I found myself in a dark forest. In my fear, I had labored in sin, with no love for mankind. Until brother sun illuminated my soul and I came back to the Father who forgave me my debts". Although I was forgiven; I was left to deal with my sins. I had a lot to work through before I could serve the Lord! In a way, I was like Moses who was held back from entering into the Promised Land! I was powerless to change anything about my life. The hell of it is that I couldn't change anything, no matter what I did! I kept coming back to where I started. I found myself alone and abandoned. I was living in a vacuum. A nowhere man! I spent so much time alone that I came to accept it. Like someone who comes to accept a disability and gets on with their life. I accepted loneliness as a way of life for me! But, emptiness is something different. Emptiness is for me the need to serve a purpose. Being in the midst of change and like the Prodigal Son I was worn out, depressed, fatigued and I was feeling lonely, and ugly! I had no money, no clothes. In general, I had no life!

I struggled to get up and begin again! I began writing bits and pieces in my journal and I began to work through my depression. I would go straight to my computer and work; so that no time would be wasted staring into space wishing I were slim and rich! Why would I like to be slim? Because, someone would be attracted to me! Why rich? Because I could have the power to change! I know it is wrong to want these things because each of them represents a superficial world. Writing became an essential part of my existence. I planned to write my way out of my poor existence, and into a purpose and a future. "Delight yourself in the Lord, and He shall give you the desires of your heart." Psalms 37:4 This was God's promise to me! The desire of my heart was to find true love and serve the Lord! I wanted to love and be loved, and have a partner in serving the Lord. I have found neither! I'm not only poor but also overweight. What man could have any more anchors on him? There is no way out! Everything I try comes to failure. What makes things worse is that I have and continue to try to live my life as a Christian yet I have lost everything I ever had! I always felt a calling and felt someday God would open a door and all the suffering would have had purpose! Job in the Bible and I are the same. I have nothing left to give! Nobody knows the frustration and hurt of rejection, powerlessly watching your ex-wife leaving you seeking another man that can offer her a better life. All I can do is write about my life but I can't change anything. Every effort ends in failure. The hole is just too deep to climb out of. It is very, very frustrating. I have been feeling so empty! My stomach aches! All I see is that everything has been taken away from me! All I can see is the past, I'm stuck, I'm locked in the present and all I can see is loss and pain. I have been feeling really guilty for not having any money nor life to give Nathan. I continue to go to the church in hopes that in God someday I will find my place, yet one door after another closes in my face. This too is very frustrating. I am a prisoner, what crime have I committed?

My only hope is in the Lord! The Lord's words to me yesterday where Jeremiah 29:11 "I have a plan for your life. It is a plan for good and not for evil. It is a plan to give you a future and a hope." I am really struggling with direction in my life and I have been depressed and haven't been sleeping. I really need to know what to do! My true hearts desires are to find love and mostly to be in the Lord's service. Depression makes it difficult! I have no ambition! I'm having a hard time writing because I don't feel like I'm a whole person without love and I feel like I need to do more than just write about it!

Then in a dream the Lord encouraged me! I was on a big white boat, ocean liner, with no windows. I had the cabin right in front of the ship and I opened the door to see icebergs; I felt the ship was moving too fast in open waters. We were on our way to the Bahamas. I felt danger. At first this dream seemed just a simple dream but the dream stayed with me and I began to think there was more to it. At first I thought the dream was a warning that I was heading into danger but then I thought, "who is driving the big white boat, a boat with no windows like Noah's Ark?" It was God! I am in this boat or this is my situation in life! The Lord is quickly bringing me through these dangerous waters to the Bahamas (Paradise). The Lord is taking me swiftly through these necessary dangerous waters of the development of my life. Jesus, the Living Waters, the ocean teaming with life and the symbol of abundant life! I am on a journey and will pass through these dangerous waters but the Lord is steering the ship and I will have trust, be patient and confident in the Lord.

Then, like at the end of the dark forest, there was a sense of working out my life and direction! Tough times are learning times! I have been very happy lately. I have an attitude of joy and peace within me, with nothing! This is a state I have always sought to achieve. My mother had this state of being and I always admired her for it. She had nothing yet she had a peace about her that came from God. No one has inspired me more than my mother. I was soon to discover that St. Francis was of this nature as well! Jesus said: "Blessed are the poor"! I have discovered a power in poverty, a peace in simplicity, in an uncomplicated, humble, free lifestyle! I find that scriptures make more sense to me as a poor person. I still have concerns though. I enjoy being alone but I do not enjoy being lonely.

I'm not sure how I got involved with the Divorced Healing ministry. The retreats I went to at the Catholic Separated and Divorce Healing Ministry at Mount Carmel were very helpful. Like the father forgave the prodigal Son and welcomed him home; something about me changed. Others have pointed out to me in the last while. They tell me I bring a certain energy or brightness into a room when I come and I am missed when I am not there. They tell me the group is not the same without me! Huh!

I talked to a Mediterranean lady. We talked about our faith and I told her why I came and she told me about her life and how God had given her back her life. Then Father Roger asked me to read the scriptures. Gina told me when she closed her eyes she saw me in a white robe (not brown!) and my heart was glowing! Then there was a lady who said she was afraid! I told her not to be afraid that I would pray for her! I talked to a man a couple of times and later he came up and told me he wanted to come back and talk to me about some of the things I had said. I thought, "Oh God, what did I say?" I asked him what do you mean. He said: "he didn't have a faith in thirty years and he wanted to return next week. I had told him, "The way to begin is the same way one begins a relationship with a woman!" Then the lady I told I would pray for came up to me and hugged me and thanked me for praying for her and said: "I'm going home unafraid! Like the Prodigal Son, the Father had welcomed me home and I was set to work in the Father's fields! And I, like the Prodigal Son, remembered the lost and had compassion on them!

Then I had a most unusual experience. I was taken back when I watched a movie called: "Brother Sun and Sister Moon." I cried when I saw the life of St. Francis. I saw in the life of St. Francis a life of Holy Poverty! This is what I had been seeking! The true way of serving God is in poverty and unconformity! I made a spiritual connection that day. St. Francis said: "We are just a band of brothers who love the Lord; each of us serves to our own capacity! Go into all the world and preach the Gospel; and when necessary use words!" Here were the religious ideals I had been seeking, and I began to seek after the life of St. Francis. I had a love for God! I thought it could be possible for me to spend my life in love with God. Human love had lost its interest for me. And I thought that when Nathan had grown I would try to become a brother. One day I was in my car and as I went by this particular piece of land on a hill, my mind drifted. I saw a church, with brothers and sisters in brown robes. I believe it was at that moment the Lord planted a vision of a Franciscan calling and mission in my mind and heart.

I attended Edith Stein Roman Catholic Institute and did some studies, and wrote a paper on holy poverty. I met a priest named Father Rogers. I talked to him about my interest in St. Francis and living the life of St. Francis. He told me I should join the Roman Catholic Church. I tried to fit in for 20 years. I was reluctant in trying to fit into the church again. But I wanted more of a life of commitment to Christ through the lifestyle of St. Francis. I started to attend the Lady of Scapular Church in Niagara Falls. I was told my baptism wasn't valid and so I was re-baptized and confirmed on the same day. April 6, 1996. I was 49. I began to attend the Secular Franciscan Order at St. Kevin's in Welland, Ontario. New to the Catholic Church I was asking myself if I should pray the Rosary as the others do? I had been taught not to pray to Mother Mary! I was struggling with this in my mind when all of a sudden a car slammed on the brakes in front of me, and on the back of the bumper was a sticker, "Pray the Rosary!"

Nathan and I were beginning to find ourselves! Nathan and I were doing fine. We had moved into a nicer apartment. We lived close to Marlene and Rob. Nathan could go and see his mom when he wanted on a regular basis. Nathan made friends in the neighborhood. Some are still his friends today. He often refers back to his time in the hood! Until the Conservative Government under Mike Harris made cuts to the Father's allowance! He said, "Let them eat Kraft dinner and dented cans of Tuna!" When the cuts came I couldn't afford to live in the apartment. I had to move and was cut off social assistance again for I didn't qualify without an address! Nathan moved in with his mom and I became homeless again!

All by myself, where could I go now? I never felt lonelier! Marlene had moved on and was with Rob. Darren was married with his family, and Tara now had her own family too. I felt like I didn't have a family or friend in the world.

Feeling alone I wanted to dedicate my life to God. I wanted to become a brother. But it was not to happen. It was God's wisdom that I didn't become a brother in a monastery. Just when I thought I was no longer needed, I began to see just how much my family needed me! My family is unique. I am so grateful for my family. I am proud of all my kids; I know they all have a faith! We are a close family. Since we traveled so much we developed a close family bond, for all we had was each other! We had no friends, no one we could trust but each other. We have become more than family we became trusted travelers through life. I felt I needed to be there for them! Marlene always complains about everything but when it comes down to it she is one of the most generous persons I have ever known. She is always there to help and give of herself. And that is all that really matters in the end. Darren was always there to help as well! Darren had rented another store. He wanted to turn it into a corner grocery store. He let me move into the back of the store.

While I was living in the store I met the owners of the building who were Filipino. They saw my guitar and asked me if I was Roman Catholic. "Yes, I am!" I replied. They asked if I could come and play the guitar and sing at their Catholic Charismatic Prayer Group. I had spent so much time alone I was really withdrawn within myself. That prayer group started me on a journey of courage. And so, with my social anxiety and panic attacks, I began to play for them. The Filipino people were good to me and as each week went by I grew more comfortable.

I had a dream: I saw a little boy crying over a picture of his father and I felt in my heart sadness for that boy for he was missing his dad. I then received a call from Ann telling me that Dad had been kicked out of the house because he had molested Melissa. She continued to tell me how he was sleeping in the car and how Steve her husband picked him up and took him for a coffee and then to a motel. Ann then took him to the hospital; for he had just broken down.

The next day I picked up my dad from Ann's. He told me he had gotten himself in big trouble. He was very remorseful and crying and ashamed. Dad had been lonely, and after mom died he hooked up with a lady that was younger than him. She was a big lady and looked a little or perhaps she reminded him of mom and he married her. She had a fully grown, slightly retarded daughter. Dad told me the daughter felt lonely and left out and would come into their bed; somehow they all were intimate together. Dad told me he thought he was showing the girl love and she was happier when they were intimate. His wife felt guilty about the situation and had my dad arrested. As we sat there together we talked about God and how he could begin the healing when we ask him to forgive us. I turned on a religious tape (Don Moen) before I went into the bathroom for my bath and when I came out of the bathroom my dad was crying and he claimed God came over him. He claimed he was forgiven! Monday March 3, 1997.

I made the decision to move out of the store and my father and I moved into an apartment together. It was decided that this one bedroom would be my father's and I would stay to help him for a couple of months. My father loved Noreen and tried to make things right but was arrested for making contact with her and spent the night in jail. He went to court and was sentenced to two years in jail and I am sure it was because of his faith he survived it. I would go to see my dad in jail and after when he had his own apartment. All alone and suffering from diabetes my dad would cry when I told him I loved him.

I felt sorry for my Dad; he was very happy for a while. After mom died he sold the house and took a trip to Hawaii. He had gotten married again. I read the scriptures at their wedding. They all were happy together. Dad loved playing Santa Clause at the Pen Center each year. Dad was generous and made Christmas goods for everybody. But, he had lost it all. I felt disappointed in myself for I felt I had let him down for when he was getting on in years his car broke down and he couldn't afford to get it fixed and he was stuck in the apartment. He asked me if I thought it was time for him to give up his license and forget about the car and driving. I regret I agreed with him! Dad was a good driver all his life and perhaps if he could have gotten out to garage sales and picking up junk and fixing it he would have lived longer!

I attended a retreat at St. Augustine's House. While I was on my way home Marlene called me on my cell phone and told me my father had died. He had hit his head in the bathroom, a result of Diabetes. I was expected to make the arrangements and with the help of the Canadian Legion, who blew the last call for my dad, performed the funeral service for my father. I remember the good times, especially when Dad and I went scuba diving on a wreck close to Christian Island. On our way back to shore the waves where rough and dad fell over and couldn't get up for the water was pushing him down. He cried out for help. I rushed over to him, and pulled him to shore. Dad found on the wreck a piece of wood with a rod through it. It looked just like an anchor. Dad gave it to Livinia and she gave it to me and I keep it as a memorial of my dad.

CHAPTER SEVEN

"Ordained and Homeless"

I ENJOYED MY time with the Filipino Charismatic group. I met a good Filipino man named Paco, he and I became good friends; we talked a lot about the Lord. He told me how unhappy he was and said, "He didn't want to wake up in the morning!" He took me to a healing prayer meeting in Toronto. And on the way home his wife was angry with him because I was too big for their van and cost extra gas! A short time later I am sad to say, Paco died in his sleep! I also met a Filipino lady named Zenaida at the prayer group and we became good friends. Zenaida met my dad and would visit with me when I visited my dad in jail. Prompted by the Holy Spirit she told me I was to look after my dad and show him love. After Dad went to jail I was homeless and she let me sleep on the couch in her front room on and off. The other times I stayed with my daughter, Tara and Willie. I had to do something. I applied for welfare and made an application for Niagara Housing.

I spent the next couple of years attending church and just sitting on the bench trying to find my place within the Roman Catholic tradition. I was there to serve! I attended the "Called by Name Program" and made an application for ministry to the vocations director. Zenaida and I attended the third Order of St. Francis together and were accepted into the order at the same time. The third order Franciscans where all good people. But, I was different, I had seen too much. They functioned within the box, but I realized I functioned outside the box! To me, that was the true calling of St. Francis. I visited a Fr. Celestine, a Franciscan Brother. He told me I should have begun earlier in my life. I thought if I couldn't fit into the Franciscan Order perhaps other orders might except me. I spent a little time with the Good Shepherd brothers in Hamilton. I went back to the vocations director a few years later to find my application sitting in a filing cabinet. They had not even considered my application at all.

I attended another Roman Catholic Filipino Charismatic event in Toronto. I had been asked to tell my testimony. I was asked if I could let them see the testimony and when I began to read it, it wasn't the one I had written, it had been changed to fit into the program. At one point the lights went low and a mist came upon the crowd and the chant of speaking in tongues filled the air. They felt that it was very important to them that I should speak in tongues as well! But, for me it didn't happen! When I returned home that night I woke up speaking in tongues. I had these syllables of this unknown language on my mind. I returned to a Living Waters Prayer Group I had been attending previously before going to the event in Toronto. The person sitting in the pew in front of me began speaking in tongues. It was the same language I had heard a few nights before! I then recognized my mind had copied the same syllables as one who remembers a song!

I took another trip to Toronto to a Catholic Charismatic Conference. On the way back someone asked me if I enjoyed myself. I said, "Oh yes!" But without missing a beat I said: "I'm not going to go anymore!" I was full. I now needed to give of myself! I was well overdue. I was compelled to give of myself. I was done with words. I couldn't wait any longer, I felt like I would burst. I was compelled by the words of St. Francis: "Go into all the world and preach the Gospel; if necessary use words!" I was going nowhere in the Roman Catholic Church! It was the same old story and I became discouraged again!

It was not long after that, I was looking in the yellow pages for a Franciscan Church to attend and came across St. Francis Christ Catholic Church. I called and attended the mass on Sunday. It was a small church. Once when the elderly priest held up the host during the Eucharist, I heard a voice within me that say: "Help him Larry!" I didn't realize in the beginning but this church was an Old Catholic Church and not under Rome. My direction was about to change when I met the person of Pastor Del Baier. My lady Filipino friend didn't like it that I was attending another denomination. After that my Roman Catholic lady friend began to reject me and told me she would not marry me! I agreed with her that if God wanted me to be in the Roman Church I would go to the Roman Catholic Bishop and ask him what I should do. When I went to see him, he listened to my story and told me to write all this down and drop it off to him; he said he would assign me a spiritual director. I did all that he told me, I handed the letter in personally.

While I was at the office and I had handed in my story I noticed the lady who was in charge of the annulment was there! Perhaps, she said something to the Bishop or could it be that I am too old? I never understood why but I never got any reply! It might have been that when I first went to the "called by name program" I might have been blackballed from the beginning for I did speak up to the Bishop at that time about something I don't remember but I think that set my fate! What a waste of precious years! I waited for a phone call, a letter, but nothing! He simply didn't respond! This seems to be the way the church deals with these things they just don't respond. Their words mean nothing! He simply ignored me! In fact, no one really seemed to care! Not one person asked me why I was considering leaving the Roman church! After that I seemed to be black balled! Any attempt to join anything Roman Catholic proved unsuccessful. Too bad. I believe I could have made a good deacon, one who would have reached out to the lost and brought them back to the church!

I began to attend St. Francis Church. The Father was a marvelous man and a spiritual father to me. One Saturday I attended St. Francis and Christ Catholic Church picnic. To my surprise Bishop Mullen told me he wanted me to attend the St. Luke's Cathedral the next day at 9:30 a.m. For he was going to induct me into the Order of St. Francis of Assisi as a brother and the next day I was inducted as brother Larry in the New Order of St. Francis; by the good Archbishop Reverend Donald Mullen; it took a while for it to sink into my head, I was a Franciscan Brother! My greatest desire had come true. I planed on remaining a brother for the rest of my life and continue to study and be ordained as a deacon; as brother Francis was! I had another meeting with Bishop Mullen to discus my vision of a Franciscan Ecumenical Community Mission. I began to live as a Franciscan brother. O Lord, and Father Francis bless me and guide me.

I had the opportunity to begin theological studies at St. Mary's Seminary. Previously I had only achieved a grade five education. And, recently I had completed first year at Waterloo University. I had learned to write essays at the writing clinic at the University. Since I was to studying theology I decided at the same time to return to adult school. I was 52 years old and I completed my basic education and completed grade 8, and my grade 12 diplomas and completed a Diploma of Sacred Theology. In a way I was glad that I had not received the traditional education. I needed to experience life. I had gained an empirical education. I had learned from my own experiences through life! I was lucky to find my purpose in life; many never find their purpose or destiny!

St. Francis church was a small parish and I had an opportunity to grow in ministry. Every Sunday I began picking up and bringing people to St. Francis Church. Father Del was very patient with me and made every effort to help me along the journey. It was at this time my back was beginning to give me trouble. It was getting that I couldn't stand for any length of time without experiencing pain. We often went on retreat to St. Augustine's House a monastery in Michigan. I was so grateful for the opportunity to make steps towards serving the Lord. In my first act of service I assisted Fr. Del when we baptized Tara's son, Joshua.

As Brother Larry I began to play my guitar and sing each Sunday night at St. Francis Church. I eventually was ordained a Deacon. I performed the Vesper Service and preached the Gospel each Sunday night. I began the St. Francis Thrift Store with the idea of helping to support St.

Francis Church. The Father was retiring and it was assumed that I would prepare to pastor St. Francis Church. My son, Darren, and his father-in-law Stan together, built the St. Francis thrift Store. I was beginning to feel good about myself. My brother Richard and I painted the whole church and put up a steeple. The mayor of Niagara Falls attended the ceremony of the steeple mounting.

A lady that visited the thrift store summoned me to the hospital to attend to her dying father. The man was in a coma and had been an atheist throughout his life. The family gathered around the man and we all prayed for him. His son stayed with the man throughout the night and the man woke up and was shouting fire, fire, and then he began to tell the story to his son about how Jesus had taken him to hell and asked him if he wanted to stay there. Jesus in his grace gave the man the opportunity to be saved. The man died during the night and the son related the story to me at which I told during the funeral and burial service. The mother remarked how my music had blessed her.

I lived in the back of the store and I slept on the green garbage bags of donated clothes. I had hoped the store would have worked out but the cost of the rent overtook the income. And again, the social services found out I had a business and they cut my income off. I finally gave the entire contents away for free and moved out. Stories were that I sold all the clothes and took off with the money. There seem to be many false murmurings about me going back to Archbishop Mullan! I began to feel a negativity growing towards me. The church had been donating me money for gas money to get the people back and forth to church for morning and evening services. The donation was discontinued and it made it impossible for me to continue picking up the people. I was not to become the pastor of St. Francis Church. I left after I had a frightful dream of warning! I dreamt that an evil force emanating out of the communion Tabernacle box was pulling me in! Eventually the church was closed and became an apartment building. Feeling discouraged I felt I needed to spend more time going away from establish traditional religion and again I felt I needed to return back to time when the early Christians broke bread in their homes. To the time before the churches became institutionalized!

My brother Richard introduced me to a man from Indonesia. We decided together to build a chapel in his motel. Brother Richard and I worked hard on the Chapel. Darren got Michele's father to build a pulpit, altar and baptism fount, and a good friend of mine built a stain glass window. Father Del came to my rescue again and he introduced me to a bishop in the Old Catholic Tradition and Bishop Polen came and with all good intention consecrated the new Chapel of Divine Mercy on December 3, 2000 and ordained me to the priesthood. I was 53 year old. He also blessed Sister Lilly at the same time as a sister in the Order of St.Francis. My father and family attended the service!

Unfortunately, the Motel owner was thinking of a wedding chapel to make money on weddings for himself and that wasn't my intentions! I came at Christmas Eve with the intentions of performing a Christmas service. I came with gifts in hand and the man blew up at me, "How dare you disrupt me and my family!" I cancelled the Christmas service. Since we did such a good job of turning the room into a chapel he decided he could make money with the room by renting it. Then he asked me to move the chapel into the basement, which I did. I don't know why I moved it, I probably still hung onto hope it would work out. After

I moved the entire chapel the owner sent damaging e-mails to Bishop Pollen in California and I received a letter from the e-mail saying I was excommunicated! After it didn't work out and after that experience I swore the next time I would do it on my own! I had wasted too much time simply trying to belong. From now on I will leave my life in God's hands. Jesus and I would have to find our own way. I needed to create my own identity!

Since I resigned from the Old Catholic Church, Zenaida was more accepting of me and was kind enough to let me sleep on her couch again. I took a Driver Instructors Course in Toronto and hitched a ride with one of the students. I had feelings for her and might have gotten married if I had returned to the Catholic faith. We attended Cana a marriage preparation course together. I was also helping her with immigration lawyers to stay in the country at the time and perhaps that had something to do with why she wanted to attend Cana. I had many questions about the Roman Catholic Church. I couldn't follow along in blind-faith as Zenaida! I had a dream: At the end of her sidewalk was a white picked fence with a white gate. I saw a blind lady leaving and closing the gate. The message was clear to me. My blind faith had now left me! Often I would try and talk with her about the faith but in her mind she was right and I was wrong, period!

After I took the course and passed I received my Driver Instructors License and reluctantly began working at a driving school in the city. But I couldn't get over that I still was a priest! That was where my heart was. I performed a baptism for the Driving School owner. In time I bought my own used car and opened my own driving school called: Goodnough's Defensive Driving School. Nathan met a new girlfriend at St. Thomas Adult School where he was upgrading. Nathan moved out from his mom's and Nathan and Lacey and I moved into an apartment together. It was good to be together again and back with family.

It wasn't long before my driving school car began to wear down and I began to wear down! Driving Instruction proved to be too difficult for me and I began to be gripped by panic attacks and back pain. I could work no more. My doctor agreed. I had no choice; my doctor wrote a letter that I was unable to continue working. I again applied for welfare. It had been a few years since I had applied for housing but thank God they had a place for me. It couldn't have come at a better time! I had no way to survive anymore. I was so happy and thankful! I have a place of my own I could call home. I was in a mess. I was feeling anxiety daily. The good doctor offered me drugs for my anxiety, but I turned them down. I don't even take aspirins! One can understand that after my bad drug experience I have a phobia for taking drugs. If you are an individual and the world thinks there is something wrong with you, the most common cure for anxiety is to dope you up with drugs and send you back to work! Nathan was sent to a psychologist and when he went for the visit the doctor wanted to stuff Nathan with pharmaceutical drugs. Nathan refused to take them and the doctor threw Nathan out of the office when he told the doctor he was nothing more than a legal drug pusher!

CHAPTER EIGHT

"Evils of Evils"

LIFE HAD TAKEN its toll on me! I was tired and I was battling depression and anxiety attacks and chronic back pain! But something even worse was happening to me! For some time I had been experiencing a deep fear that came from the depth of my soul! This was different than a panic attack! When it came it separated me from the material realm. Yet, I was fully aware. It came like a dark angel and stabbed me in my heart. My heart felt crushed by the presence of the most awful, vile, evil of evils! Most of the time I was fine, but some days were worse than others. It may not happen for months. Then I will go through a couple of days were I would have numerous attacks in one day. It even attacked me in my sleep and dreams, and wakes me up calling out to Jesus to save me. It would come upon me unexpectedly. Once, I was standing in the kitchen, my family doesn't understand why I am taking so long, I don't let on, and I hide it and try to act normal. But, all of a sudden, I am in a different realm, the world is silent and everything becomes in slow motion! It is a feeling that something is going to happen, something awful. There is a numbness and rush that hits me in the back of my neck, and then goes straight to my heart like a knife that pierces my soul with feelings of guilt, and shame, and real pain! I am affected physically; it makes me gage, and I dry vomit.

I couldn't figure this out; it was different than the fear that came when one has a panic attack. I had experienced that in the past. This was different! It took me a while to understand this fear. The answer came to me one day in the midst of an attack when I began to pray immediately to the Lord to "take this cup from me!" I began to realize I was repeating the words of Jesus in his agony in the garden at the Mount of Olives! He was in so much agony. He sweated drops of blood! (Luke 22:42-44) I realized that I was sharing in Jesus' suffering so that I will never forget the pain and the fear, all the vilest, and shameful sins of the world, Jesus took upon himself, the price He paid for me! Even his Father couldn't look upon him on the cross! It finally dawned on me, my constant prayers each morning was: "Lord be in my all, Lord be in me, through me and around me!" I didn't know what I was asking for when I asked Jesus to be in my all! The disciples asked a similar question when they wanted to sit at the right hand of Jesus. Jesus said: "You don't know what you are asking!" when you love someone, you want to share in their life, you become one. You share the good and the bad! There is no doubt, the Spirit of Jesus lives within me! (Col 1:27) I am a totally different person than I was before Jesus came into my life. My heart for the most part is filled with the love of God for all people. Often my heart overflows into fighting back tears, with an overpowering love for God and compassion for others. I remember dreaming about Jesus being scourged at the pillar. In the dream the sun was very bright and I was a prisoner. And I yelled out my prison window "Don't do that to him he has done nothing wrong, do that to me instead!" I had another dream I was in an arena, the devil was hurting kids, I yelled at him, try that on me, and the devil began chasing me, I ran into a house, and on the stand in the hall was a steel comb. The devil began to bang the door down and I was stabbing him with the handle of the comb! I want to share in Jesus' suffering that kind of sacrificial life exists within me! God is within me, would I not feel peace and joy and tremendous love, but would I not also feel the agony of the sins he took upon himself in the Garden? With my suffering with Christ I have also assurance. I will also share in his glory and assurance of the resurrection with Jesus in heaven. Once the fear served its purpose; the fear left me! In Jesus I saw a love like no other, a love great and strong, enough to give his life for another!

I found from experience that when I felt anxiety coming on I would have a few beers for medicinal purposes. The doctor agreed that I was disabled and unable to work. I was diagnosed with Phobic Anxiety Disorder with Panic attacks, Obsessive Compulsive Disorder, with Morbid Obesity, Hypertension and Diffuse Joint Pain and Degenerate Arthritis. I applied for a disability pension and I was denied. I appealed the decision from disability and I was accepted. When I first went to the doctors, he weighed me at three hundred and thirty three pounds. The highest I got was 373lbs. Later, I discovered I had not only high blood pressure but also I was diabetic and with the pain in my back I couldn't stand up for any longer than a few minutes and I had to rely on an electric scooter to get around. I reluctantly took the blood pressure and diabetic pills. I couldn't take the pills they made me lethargic! I didn't want to be part of the pharmaceutical complex. In time, I changed my eating habits and began drinking distilled water and limited the amount of beer I drank, lost some weight and stopped taking the pills. But, when I went to visit Doctor Fernandez I thought he might throw me out of his office when I told him I quite all of the pills! But he was very patient with me and realized I had a phobia of taking drugs! I told him I didn't want to be any part of a eugenics program! He explained to me that it is not just about keeping the sugar levels down but that I had a metabolic problem and needed to take the diabetes medicine and my high blood pressure pills and assured me I would loose weight if I kept on the pills. I lost 14 pounds but I couldn't loose any more no matter what I did. I tried everything and even considered by pass surgery. To be honest, it has given me hope for the one desire of mine that has not been fulfilled is to find a companion and find love in my life; but no body wants to love a fat guy!

I have always struggled with conditional love and human love! A common theme in my dream is of a beautiful lady, dressed in white, like a Greek goddess. Like someone you would see in Greek mythology. She had long sandy blonde hair wavy/curly hair tied back on the sides. She had a strong face, Roman nose. In my dream she was on my left side and she leaned forward and kissed me. I could see in her face she really cared and loved me. Was this an Angel, letting me know her presence! Or perhaps the deepest desire of my heart! It is certainly obvious that human love is conditional but when you see a woman with a couple of kids you can see why! But this also means that the man also has the right to be conditional. Friends remain in a state of unconditional love but when that friendship crosses into a sexual relationship it then becomes a conditional relationship, and rightly so. I can now see why St. Francis didn't get married for he wanted to remain in the unconditional love of God rather than the conditional love of humans. Also, in possessions one enters into the earned conditional love of mankind but in poverty one remains in the unconditional love of God.

I got through the most difficult times in my life by literally writing out my feelings and analyzing myself. I wrote my heart out, it was my way of talking to God. My journal was one of emotions and I poured my feelings out! I worked out my fears and tears, feelings and emotions, pain and depression, weaknesses and strengths. I wrote from November 1990 though to July 2002. I wrote for nine years and seven months and then I suddenly stopped! There was nothing more to say! I literally wrote myself well! Without prescription drugs! I searched myself and got to know myself, my dreams, hopes and my strengths and weaknesses. I learned that my worst enemy was myself! But I'm not such a bad guy after all. For the most part I was at peace with myself. Living in the present and in the presence and trusting in God but, I had to take time for myself or I wasn't going to be around.

I got a call from Lana's son David. He came and spent a little time with me. He was having some mental issues and needed some background to help himself. It was then that I found out that Lana had committed suicide by jumping into Niagara Falls. Talking to David, I realized that this mental illness was part of my family genetics. I wish I had known my sister, Lana, more but I only got to meet her a few times, once in a train station. A few years later, we had a remembrance ceremony for Lana at Niagara Falls.

CHAPTER NINE

"Coming Into My Own"

THANK GOD, I was now in a position that I didn't have to worry about surviving daily. This was the first time in my entire life I had some security. Security was the first step to begin healing. I had only one experience with the Disability that they cut me off, but I appealed it and was reinstated! Housing has restored my trust in government to do what is right. I became homebound! I began to realize how my mother felt! No one can understand the feelings unless you have experienced the rejection, the aloneness and how unloved one feels when one is overweight and society rejects you, women reject you, and the church rejects you. One would think that in a church, a person would find acceptance and unconditional love but what I experienced was more guilt upon me by adding gluttony to my list of faults. I wished I could belong to a church and serve a good purpose but the reality is that I couldn't.

I know that belonging to society is unrealistic and from my previous experience with the church I have come to the conclusion that it is best not to belong but rather to set myself apart from the culture, and not be part of the conformity.

I found that my studies at the different denominations beneficial. I will not reject any denomination, all have truth, and all love our savior. According to each of them they are the true church. Each church ideal was re-enforced by the circle, and you cannot belong to the circle, if your thoughts are outside the circle! I began to think differently, I read: "The most high does not dwell in temples built with human hands!" Acts 7:48 I was beginning to think Jesus also would prefer to be on Main Street rather than in the church. In all my searching for a church to belong to, it finally came to me that they weren't interested in me! They were interested in their own kind, their own class, someone who would contribute to the church and be part of the neighborhood.

I spent a lot of time alone in thought and prayer in my new apartment. I built a chapel. I prayed often for self-conquest but in the end I came to accept myself for who I was. God loves me just as I am. In my writings I know my weaknesses. I am a person who needs a purpose in life. I learned that I usually become depressed when I feel like I am not accomplishing anything. I learned to accept myself, for who I am. I accepted that I was born counter cultural. But by the grace of God I am what I am, and by his grace within me was not without effect. As the apostle Paul has said: No, I worked harder than all of them – yet not I, but the grace of God that was with me. 1Corinthians 15:10 I learned to be happy and live each moment in thankfulness. In time, I began to have the courage to challenge my own self and pushed myself to test my social anxieties and I learned my limitations and the panic attacks didn't come as often. My apartment became my monastery and my hermitage. I meditated and prayed often, giving thanks to God for my apartment and I began to recuperate gaining strength by being alone with God! I started living as a Franciscan brother. I needed my time alone; it was not without purpose. It gave me the time to find myself and to know myself. A quote from Paul Tilich says it best. "Our language has wisely . . . created the word "loneliness" to express the pain of being alone. And it has created the word "solitude" to express the glory of being alone.

Each morning I would awake and go into my chapel and thank the Lord for the new day and take communion. I began to feel full as I had before! During one of my morning prayers I felt wrong for keeping the communion to myself. I felt I needed to become the church to those who didn't have a place to belong! And, I felt the need to return to the early church and begin again! The love of God compelled me to go back to those who needed the saving love of God. I knew that there would be those who would criticize me for my weaknesses but it is not about me, it is about Jesus! The greatest deception of the devil is convincing us that he is not real and there is something wrong with us. Since I dedicated my life to the Lord this would be his tactics! God, who loves me enough to give his son for my sins, would help me to find a way for me to minister to those who need his love as well.

Then, finally I found myself feeling good again. I remember stopping for a moment and saying to myself, I'm happy! I have sincerely reached that point, where I can say I have: "inner peace within myself." I have nothing! I own nothing! But, I'm happy. I'm anchored in empirical experience of Jesus. "I sought the Lord and He heard me, and delivered me from all my fears." Psalms: 34:4 (KJV) I wasn't going to find a church to fit into, for they were one and the same. I couldn't fit their image of the middle class Jesus. I began to look for an alternative church. My thoughts went out to those who didn't fit into the established church. I felt I needed to become the church to those who didn't have a place to belong! I felt the need to return to the early church and begin again! I felt it would be selfish of me to keep the body and blood of Christ to myself. I felt I needed to bring the communion to the people who are outside the box. I have always felt that God intended me to work with the poor, and all that proceeded was an empirical time of preparation. My experience as a child, my time on the streets, my time in the Children's Aide, and Reform School created in me a social justice kind of attitude. I cherish my experiences I had with each of the denominations. I am part of every denomination I attended. I saw good in each of them. I remember all the saints I met along the way. But, my heart was not with the established church. I belong among the poor, the needy, and the outcast. I decided to rise above it all, forgive all, and leave all behind and begin a new positive life.

My thoughts and my calling were confirmed when I read this parable of Jesus: "Suppose one of you has a hundred sheep and loses one of them. Doesn't he leave the ninety-nine in the open country and go after the lost sheep until he finds it? And when he finds it, he joyfully puts it on his shoulders and goes home. Then he calls his friends and neighbors together and says, 'Rejoice with me; I have found my lost sheep.' I tell you that in the same way there will be more rejoicing in heaven over one sinner who repents than over ninety-nine righteous persons who do not need to repent!" Luke 15: 3-7

I began to think how I might begin an Order of St. Francis to reach those shut-in or for some reason didn't fit into the church. I was not out to draw a line between those in and outside the church. I simply thought that there would be those who would be blessed also living the life style of St. Francis. Yet, I had to abandon some of the Franciscan groups I encountered who where too connected to the established church to be truly Franciscan in my mind.

Once again God lead me and encouraged me when Father Del introduced me to a fine group of Christians, the International Lutheran Fellowship. The name was later changed to the Lutheran church – International. I was impressed with Martin Luther. Luther was at home with the common man; at home in the seminary or in a bar. But, would they understand my calling or me? I filled out an application and on October 31, 2002, I was received into the Ministerium of the International Lutheran Fellowship and roistered as a priest. I was overjoyed when I received a "Letter of Call" to begin a specialized Ministry to serve the Church Universal according to Franciscan Values and the Lutheran Confession to those currently outside the formal fellowship of the church. January 19, 2003.

I love the Lord! For everything that is beautiful and good is of God. One's purpose and focus should be on what you love! Feeling inspired and an overwhelming desire to bring faith, hope, and charity to a hurting world and wanting to live the simple life of St. Francis. I began to visit the poorer retirement homes in the area performing regular evening services on Sunday night, playing and singing with my guitar. Nathan and Sister Lily would accompany me at the homes. It was a fun time. I remember one time, I asked Nathan to hand out the communion to the elderly for they couldn't line up as in the church. I had the lights low and had lighted candles. I was playing my guitar to compliment the communion. As Nathan began to give out the communion one lady had palsy and would sway back and forth and so Nathan looked at me to know what to do. He then got into the same rhythm with the lady and fired the communion into her mouth like a Frisbee. I was watching Nathan and my guitar got to close to the candles and caught on fire. What a night! Sister Lily laughed her head off! I knew I was doing what was right. I knew I was on the path of Jesus. It is not I but the grace of God working in me. I was where I was meant to be, I had empathy with their loneliness, their anxiety, their mental illness, and I was one with them, in faith, love and hope.

I was looking for a place to rent to begin my ministry. I noticed that the Emmanuel Catholic Church I had been married in years before had a space for rent. The church had been sold and turned into a Unitarian Church. Darren and I made an appointment to see the new church authorities to rent a space to reach out into the community but they rented the space for a yoga class instead. It was strange to stand in the very spot I was married years ago. Eventually, a coordinator of one of the homes asked me to visit another home in Niagara Falls. And, eventually the basement was donated to us to build a Chapel. Prayer books were donated by the ILF. I placed an advertisement in the local newspaper and some of the local churches donated an altar and benches. My only income was disability. I used what money I had for the chapel; I collected next to nothing in the collection. I needed gas to pick people up each Sunday and take them to church and back, for candles, the communion hosts, and communion wine. But, by some small miracles of donations, we had all those things!

The Lord graced me with a street minister named Frank Harrison who helped me to build the chapel. I made an application to International Lutheran Fellowship to begin a process of formation to establish the Order of St. Francis – Lutheran. With the support and prayers of Rev. Fr. Bill Babbitt, the order was approved by synod. Unfortunately Frank died before he got to see the first eight brothers and sister inducted into the Order. On the Octave of St. Francis" October 11. 2006 The Right Rev. Dr. Bishop A. Bougher consecrated the chapel, the Franciscan Lutheran Community Chapel and I was professed brother and commissioned Fr. Superior of the Order and Rev. Fr. Bill Babbitt was professed brother and commissioned as Fr. Superior of the Order of St. Francis – Lutheran USA. I made an application for Non-Profit Charity and on October 7, 2008 we were accepted as a registered charity and an application has since been made to perform marriages and established as a legal church. I now had everything I needed to begin my own ministry and the Franciscan Lutheran Community Ministry had begun.

It was around this time my Filipino lady friend from the Catholic Healing Ministry and her husband somehow didn't have a place to move into when they came back from Florida. They asked me to help, so I contacted my landlord and got them an apartment to move into to. At the same time I met a Filipino lady from Alberta through a correspondence website. We communicated back and forth and decided to meet each other. Finally she decided she would come and stay for a while. I thought it would be good to introduce here to my Filipino friend and husband thinking they would make her feel more at home. To my surprise my friend began to discredit me. She told my new friend I was poor, and basically a bum and convinced her to move back to Alberta. This is the friend I have helped, but now turned on my family and me. I'm not sure why, perhaps because I had converted to Lutheranism. Once, I was talking to her husband about the Lord and she said; I would only listen to a catholic Priest, my response was "God doesn't show favoritism!" I heard her say one time my own people are more important to me than a friend! My friend went back to Alberta but we continued to communicate with each other and in time she thought she would come and try again. I told her this time if you come, you have to be serious and get married. She agreed. I sold my old car and took the bus for three days and then turned right around with Cecilia and headed back to Ontario. We decided to have a sacramental marriage; this is when the union is blessed in a ceremony; but not registered. We intended to get married legally in time.

The International Fellowship welcomed her with open arms and she was voted in as vice-president. She didn't do anything with it. She was from a prosperity Gospel fundamentalist background, and her and I got into many disagreements. When she took my picture of mother Mary down from my chapel and repainted the room and made it into her bedroom I knew I was in trouble. Cecilia was a social climber! I was not a social climber. Cecilia and I began growing apart, especially perhaps because of her cultural upbringing. I was quite concerned about how Cecilia listened and did whatever others said. For example, another Filipino friend of hers asked me if I would come and bless her new home. The woman of the house whispered something to my friend and she in turn reached out and pulled my clerical collar off my neck! I realized then that this woman didn't have a mind of her own and was going to do whatever the Filipinos told her! When my Filipino friend and her husband found out we had gotten married they convinced her to move out again saying this is not a legal marriage! She moved into her own apartment but we continued to see each other. I would drive her to work, and for groceries for it was cold walking in the snow. One day the Filipino and her husband visited her and praised her on how well she was doing and she didn't need me. They saw my picture on her desk and were angry with her for seeing me.

Upon return from her trip to the Philippines she ignored me. I assume that her family told her to find someone who had more money for she was supporting the family in the Philippines. And in her defense, because I was receiving disability any money that she would make a certain portion was deducted from us and discouraging her from working full time or overtime without hope of advancing together! My relationship with Cecilia didn't bring me any peace, in fact; our time together brought me tremendous stress. I saw her a few times after that and then nothing.

I learned from my experience with the woman that it is important that a woman accepts you for who you are. And the same goes for one's congregation or class system, otherwise when they don't believe in what you're doing they will have no respect for you. One has to be themselves! If a woman is about money and you're not, she will disrespect you. I experienced this about my Filipino my ex-friend and her husband, people who have a value system different from ones own, will deem you unworthy and disrespect you. Once in better times my friend Gloria told me I needed to find a pickle jar kind of girl. Because once she came for supper and I gave her a pickle jar for a glass. I thought, someday I would find a lady among the Christians but every time I found a rose; I felt only the thorns. My love became for my Lord and my interest in women became less and less and then finally not at all, well, maybe there remained a little interest!

For the next five years I devoted myself to the chapel. It is a miracle to me that the chapel continued to function with very little help or donations. It would be impossible to mention all the events that touched my heart. I have certainly done every aspect of ministry, marriages, baptisms, hospital visits, funerals, counseling and encouragement, mass and music! I even got to minister to my father's wife, Noreen! She had nowhere to live and she was placed there in the home. She talked good about my dad and joked to me and called me son. There was twenty-five years difference in age between my dad and her! She was having trouble with one of the residence that kept hitting her and she remarked: "If your father was here that wouldn't happen!" Noreen never attended the chapel and I was surprised to hear she had died. By the grace of God, I had done what I set out to do; I have established the Order of St. Francis – Lutheran, and are fully equipped for ministry! Most important I have established myself, who I am, my identity, my calling not only by words alone, but also by action! But all good things must come to an end. Certain things begin to happen and I felt it was time to move on!

CHAPTER TEN

"Fulfilling a Prophecy"

MY FATHER USED to say: "A change is as good as a rest!" I went through a time of rethinking which would be the beginning of many changes. I knew I had to give up the Franciscan Lutheran Chapel and wrote a letter to Greycliff telling them that they could use the chapel anytime they wanted. I intend on spending more time on my own Chapel Divine Mercy, and my music. I intended to focus on me, for a better terminology, market myself and build on the Order of St. Francis! There is a great need! I feel I could put my services to better use by preparing men and women dedicated to God, instruments of peace, reaching out to the lost and lonely either as an individual or as a team, willing to use their gifts of ministry. I began to feel that God was leading me into something new!

I spent time writing, thinking and waiting! I accepted the fact I could no longer continue the Lord's work at the chapel. After my van broke down I found myself homebound; I accepted giving up the chapel. The good Lord sometimes has a way of ending one thing and opening the door to another. I began to spend more time on the Internet. Time at home gave me the opportunity to work on my autobiography and music with Nathan's help who without his help I would be dead in the water. I began thinking about disbanding the Order for the lack of members and interest. I felt I had no choice about keeping the order going. For it is not about numbers, it is about me! I can't change my own identity. I can't quit myself! I couldn't deny the truth about myself. To change would be to change my very being, my most true self! God has been good to me, even though the ministry hasn't been blessed with money, or great numbers of people. But, even if there were many reasons to be discouraged, I will not! I can't judge myself by worldly success! If I stop to think of my works, I would begin to analyze myself, then I would begin to compare, this is not wise. Works rather come out of the natural infilling of the Holy Spirit. It is not whom you know, what you are, or how much you do! Thinking like this leaves us feeling useless. No, I simply accept who I am! What if I don't do well in a day? What if I am unable to accomplish anything in a day? I shouldn't feel that my value lies in what I accomplished. What I accomplish will soon be forgotten! My worth is in my faith, living in the grace of God. I rest in the knowledge that I have value for just who I am! My works come out of who I am! One has to be true to oneself and follow your path not someone else's! One doesn't try to follow someone else's identity. One discovers or creates ones own identity! No one sings to the guitar, then one is a slave to the limits of the guitar! No, one plays the chords according to one's voice. Voice comes first; the guitar is subservient to the voice!

I began to think that the Franciscan Lutheran Community Ministry could become an organization with a special purpose to work outside the church but at the same time be part of it! I could see the need to build the new brothers and sisters into a body of missionaries! One that builds chapels in retirement homes, and performs a chapel service as needed, visits homes, jails, and those homebound as an evangelism team to any church!

I prayed, and began looking through the Yellow Pages and noticed a Lutheran church I had not seen before. Perhaps, I could offer my help in building up the church. I simply called the church and was surprised to receive a call back by a woman pastor! I told her I would like to talk to her and she came over and we had a good conversation. I began telling her of our Order of St. Francis and the ILF. She began to tell me how they were a small struggling church and in their meeting the night before had talked about the future of their church. Wow, God is at work! She invited me to the church's BBQ. I spent some time attending that church getting to know the people. The ILF was planning to have next year's synod in St. Catharines/Niagara Falls. The pastor had unofficially agreed to let us hold our Synod there. I had hope that eventually, the new home for the Order could be founded there! But, I received the news today that the Church would not allow us to use their building for our synod or would they allow me to have the Order of St. Francis there. Their answer was that we are of a different synod! Christ is not the problem; religion is the problem! I was reaffirmed once again that the Lord didn't want me to go in that direction!

I think there has been something wrong with religion from the beginning. The powers to be recognized that there is great power in a person who believes and follows in blind faith. Many have been taking advantage of, using God's name in vain for their own greed. But, like the saying goes: "love the sinner hate the sin." I support Christianity but not religion. Most love in my opinion today seems very shallow, based on commercialism rather than the values of the inner person or unconditional love; love has a price and when the conditions are not met, separation for a better commercial product is sought! People are consumed with commercialism; we now have commercial love, and commercial religion. There is much to know of religion and faith by researching what was left out of the bible. For example, the Gospel of Mary. Mary Magdalene was called the apostle to the apostles! Religion has turned us against each other, separated us, and caused wars, all in the name of God! All of history speaks for itself! The crucifixion of Jesus and the stoning of his brother, most of his disciples and his early followers were all killed in the name of God and religion! I don't think it is any different today. Jesus or St. Franics would not be accepted into the church today! I came to the decision. I saw no point in trying to fit into someone else's ideals of believing.

I concluded, Christianity today does not relate to me! I have stopped calling myself a Christian. In my ministry, many people I met were turned off when I said I was a Christian! But took more interest when I talked about Jesus. I have a new vision; it is the end of my religious journey and the beginning of a spiritual journey.

Interestingly, another door opened for ministry and music at a community group home of mentally challenged persons and at the same time another door has open up to do the same at an extended care facility of a hundred and fifty people. I went through a police check and when I began to work I had the same feeling as I had before of not being in the right place. I felt I just couldn't do it anymore. I thought I better just wait upon the Lord! Jesus had compassion on the people who had come a long way! Mark 8: 1-6 I remember a story of St. Francis early in his religious life when asked Sr. Claire and brother Sylvester to pray for him and ask God if he should focus his life on contemplative work or active work. Sr. Claire and bother Sylvester confirmed that Francis was to teach and preach. I find myself in this position as well. I have spent the last five years in good works but I have neither strength nor money to continue.

I retreated and stayed to myself and continued to wait on the Lord for new direction. I dreamed about a planet that was vast and beautiful. The sky was filled with stars. The planet was uninhabited except for two lone souls. The woman was fighting sleep and wanted the man to keep talking to her for she was afraid she wouldn't wake up. The woman was afraid of her own existence. The dream was about me. The planet, this world vast and beautiful and yet I feel like I am the only one on the planet. I can't fully express the feeling I felt in the dream but it was an utter emptiness, and a struggle to exist, a fear of being nothing, feeling nothing, without feeling one does not exist at all! The feelings of the woman sums up my own feelings, wanting to be heard, to exist, to be, to feel, to love, and to be fully alive!

I am beginning to realize that the ministry also would end with me. I sense that things were diminishing around me, and it is time to let go. I trust in Jesus. I know only I am forgiven and that is because of the merit of Jesus our

Lord not anything I might do! One thing is for certain, I am what I am and there is no changing me! I have often had frightening premonitions! I see them only as mile markers on the highway of life. Is what we are going to be already planned for us? How much are we in control of? I was thinking about eternal life and I had another dream. I assumed that the good go to Heaven and perhaps maybe the ones that didn't make it this time may get a chance to come back again. But then something clicked in my mind. No, the righteous are the ones who come back again to live a perpetual eternal life! The meek shall inherit the earth! Perhaps this is the new earth, and the new Heaven! I have always been a thinker, a seeker of the truth, a watcher of persons, a dreamer, and an idealist. I was becoming philosophical about life and began talking about reincarnation, genetics, and mythical stuff. I woke up to vision: I saw a mirror that was steamed over like in a shower. As the mirror began to clear I could see writing on the mirror. It was 1st Timothy 3-6! The first chapter of Timothy is about wasting time on meaningless talk about genealogies and myths!

One of the best things I ever did was to build the Chapel of Divine Mercy in my apartment! The chapel was first recognized and established and commissioned on the nineteen day of August 2005 by the Presiding Bishop the Most Rev. Dr. George Fry. The chapel is there for me whenever I need a place of worship, or just be alone with my Lord. It is scriptural: "Go into your room, and close the door and pray to your Heavenly Father". I was recently inspired to refurbish the chapel. My son and one of the brother Dan helped me to put some pews in the chapel. I'm lucky I live on the ground floor. Nathan, my son, said to me, not wanting to move the pews, asks me why do you want a chapel you could pray anywhere? He is a musician; jokingly, I asked him, would you like a music room? He said; "yes"! I said, I'm a priest; I would like a chapel! He laughed, and said nothing!

Most of the personalities I deal with seem to be much like me, introverted loners. And, so they feel comfortable praying with me privately. The Order of St. Francis often meets in the Chapel of Divine Mercy. People will drop in from time to time to take communion. I find it helpful that I have two aspects of learning and study and foundation. On one side I can explore the mystical side of St. Francis or other mystics or Gnostic Gospels and on the other side be offset and grounded in the theology of Martin Luther. From this little chapel the brothers and sisters are encouraged and trained to do their particular callings. There will always be a need for the Chapel. The chapel is beneficial in so many ways, quality not numbers is important. Numbers, power, success in this world, is the earthly way of looking at things.

God to me is the deepest desire within us to do what is holy and good. I did what I thought I was meant to do. I feel I wasted my youth and so I don't intend to retire. I intended that my elderly years would make up for my youth! There is nothing more fascinating than the life of Jesus and those Saints like Francis who where also fascinated with the life of Jesus and felt the need to live as the poor Jesus. I pray Nathan will always keep his fascination with Jesus and this mystery we have in our faith.

With Nathan's help we rebuilt our website and have gathered a sum of musical instruments and amplifiers and lately a recording studio. He has helped me put together a CD of Hymns, which I put on YouTube and I began to see the potential to reach the whole world. And, I spend more time on our website and when I realized we had seven thousand hits, people taking a look at the website I began to think of the great possibility and potential of the Internet. Many Christians throughout the world find themselves without fellowship, alone, separated from other Christians, and shut-in or homebound due to health or circumstances. These people could be reached through an Internet based Virtual Chapel. I met and ministered to many in retirement homes and when family and friends no longer needed their old computers we would donate them. It was a joy for me to see the people who feel abandoned listening to my music and coming to the website to get the latest news. Other individuals find it difficult to fit into church conformity but could be encouraged in the faith and love of our Lord through the website. Through the virtual chapel everyone is invited to become part of the family.

Then, in a moment of insight, I remembered! Thirty-three years ago and in a very stressful time in my life: I asked the Lord what I should do with my life? He gave me what I now see as a prophecy! I couldn't see it at that time, and thought how and when could this ever happen? But the Lord knew when! For all these years I kept (Psalm 96: 1-3) in my heart. And now it was the time, for the prophecy, it was now possible through the Internet.

> *Sing to the LORD a new song;*
> *Sing to the LORD, all the earth.*
> *Sing to the LORD, praise his name;*
> *Proclaim his salvation day after day.*
> *Declare his glory among the nations,*
> *His marvelous deeds among all peoples.*

This was confirmed in my mind for this is what my soul was hungering to do all along. It has been in the back of my heart and mind all of my life. The Lord's timing is different than ours! This is the desire of my heart that Jesus promised to give. Sing to the Lord! A new song; write a new song! Sing to all the earth! And do this day after day! Boldly declare the beauty of His holiness and glory, and go among the nations through the Internet, declaring stories of marvelous deeds among all peoples. This is my time of actualization, the time of my fulfillment!

I decided to resign as Father Superior in the Order of St.Francis, and the Franciscan Lutheran Community Ministry, non-profit status, and closed the ministries bank account and deleted the Franciscan Lutheran Website But, I intend to continue to be roistered a priest and brother in the Lutheran Church International and develop my YouTube channel account developing a virtual chapel and continue to write sermons and song writing and performing my music. My first concern and all that is within me is my Lord. It will be interesting to see where the Lord will take me in the future.

I don't want to forget my family. I love you all and I thank God for each one of you and pray for you daily. You have always been my closest friends and comrades. And, I will always be close by when you need me! I'll always be around! Remember we are the rich! We have been the ones who have learned the greatest lessons in life. We are the winners, we are the most blessed. As Jesus said: "Blessed are the poor"! Don't take life too serious; enjoy the life the Lord has given you. It goes by too quickly. You can't take it with you. Laugh a lot, look for humor in all things, and respect the earth and all God's creatures.

I was honored that Allissa called me uncle Larry and asked me to perform their wedding. Saying that, it was how she imagined it since she was a child! The wedding brought me full circle. It was a special time for me. I hadn't seen Marlene's family all together in twenty years! They knew me before, as the troubled young man. I was the prodigal Son, lost, deviant, confused, and without identity. But now they see the good works God had begun in me back when I accepted the Lord when I was thirty. They thought for sure I would end up in prison. But now they see me as an instrument of God, an ordained member of the clergy performing their families wedding, with no fear, standing in front of a large crowd. Some came to me later and said they were very proud of me, and for me that was my graduation! Thanks be to God!

In conclusion, I wish to thank the Lutheran Church International. January 2011 was the anniversary of my 11th year of ordination. Thank you for your confidence and trust and support in my most unusual ministry.

I wish to thank Bro. Ian Smith for his encouragement to write my autobiography. I want to say a special thanks to Sr. Skye, and Bro. Peter, Bro. Richard, Bro. Daniel, Sr. Meighan and Sr. Sue, for your love for the Lord and your desire to serve him continues to bless me. A special thanks to a street minister named Frank who was there at the beginning of the chapel construction, may Frank rest in peace. A special thanks to Michele for editing this book and a special thanks to all my family and friends and associates who helped to serve the Lord along the way.

May God richly bless you who read this book that they be encouraged in the Lord. Pray to the Lord that He would come and be in you, through you and around you. Taste and see that the Lord is good; blessed is the one who takes refuge in him. Psalm 34:8

A special thanks to you Lord Jesus, you have been closer than a brother. Thank you Lord, you never gave up on me!

All glory, honor and praise be to you Father, Son, and Holy Spirit.

Pax et bonum (Peace and all good)

CPSIA information can be obtained at www.ICGtesting.com
Printed in the USA
LVOW10s2346010715

444617LV00001BA/44/P

9 781462 891689